REALISM AND THE DRAMA OF REFERENCE:
Strategies of Representation in Balzac, Flaubert, and James

REALISM AND THE DRAMA OF REFERENCE

Strategies of Representation in Balzac, Flaubert, and James

H. Meili Steele

THE PENNSYLVANIA STATE UNIVERSITY PRESS
University Park and London

I am grateful for an Andrew W. Mellon postdoctoral fellowship at Bryn Mawr College, which helped me to complete the manuscript. My thanks go to my family and friends for their inspiration and support. Parts of this book have appeared in *Novel: A Forum on Fiction* 21, 1 (Fall 1987) (©*Novel* Corp., 1987, reprinted with permission), and *The Romanic Review* 78, 1 (1987).

Library of Congress Cataloging-in-Publication Data

Steele, H. Meili.
   Realism and the drama of reference : strategies of representation in Balzac, Flaubert, and James / H. Meili Steele.
   p. cm.
   Bibliography: p.
   Includes index.
   ISBN 0-271-00618-8
   1. French fiction—19th century—History and criticism.
2. Realism in literature. 3. Reference (Philosophy) in literature.
4. Representation (Philosophy) in literature. 5. Balzac, Honoré de, 1799–1850. Illusions perdues. 6. Flaubert, Gustave, 1821–1880. Education sentimentale. 7. James, Henry, 1843–1916. Golden bowl.
8. Literature—Philosophy. I. Title.
PQ283.S74 1988
843'.7'0912—dc19   87–22467
                                                                                    CIP

Copyright © 1988 The Pennsylvania State University
All rights reserved
Printed in the United States of America

Contents

Introduction		1
	Part One: Balzac and Flaubert	
1	Setting: Reference Beyond Signification	13
2	Speech and Knowledge: Language Without Subjects	23
3	Narrator: The Refusal of Authority	35
4	Character: Frédéric Moreau and the *Bildungsroman*	51
	Part Two: Henry James	
5	Setting: Realism Bracketed	71
6	Speech and Knowledge: The Discovery of New Referential Languages	81
7	Narrator: Reference and the Language of Being	95
8	Character: Maggie Verver's Ontological Voyage	111
	Conclusion	131
	Notes	135
	Works Cited	155
	Index	161

Introduction

The value of the offered thing, its whole relation to us, is created by the breath of language, that on such terms exclusively, for appropriation and enjoyment, we know it.[1]

—Henry James

ONE of the crucial issues of post-structuralist reflections on language is the problem of reference. Deconstruction and pragmatism have overthrown the attempts of the foundationalist and logocentric tradition to link language and the world. Language is no longer considered to be the instrument employed by the subject to locate objects; rather, subject and object become the effects of language. As Jacques Derrida says, "Subjectivity—like objectivity—is an effect of *différance*, an effect inscribed in a system of *différance*."[2] Richard Rorty, who offers a pragmatist critique of Western philosophy, also tells us that "we have to drop the notion of correspondence for sentences as well as for thoughts, and see sentences as connected to other sentences rather than the world."[3] Criticism has followed these leads and devoted itself to the deconstruction of the classic texts of realistic representation such as those of Balzac, Flaubert, and James. Roland Barthes's reading of Balzac, Jonathan Culler's of Flaubert, and John Carlos Rowe's of James,[4] to cite only three examples, illustrate how the language of realism can be unraveled, how designation is undone by metaphor, how reference becomes autoreferentiality.

This attack on traditional views of realism and representation has brought out a cry of protest about the value and coherence of what some see as a textual solipsism.[5] However, much of the protest is misdirected. Rorty's pragmatism is not a prison house of language but a behaviorism that does not take language seriously enough. "The strong textualist simply asks himself the same question about a text which the engineer or the physicist asks himself about a puzzling physical object: How shall I describe this in order to get what I want?"[6] The most notorious example of apparent nonreferentiality in contemporary criticism, Derrida's famous line "il n'y a pas de hors texte," does not deny the existence of extralinguistic forces; rather, it is a way of challenging the traditional routes of reference that posit a text over against a world.[7] As Paul de Man says of the linguistic turn in recent criticism, "What we call ideology is precisely the confusion of linguistic with natural reality, of reference with phenomenalism. It follows, that more than any other mode of inquiry, including economics, the linguistics of literariness is a powerful and indispensable tool in the unmasking of ideological aberrations."[8] Nonetheless, neither deconstruction's nor pragmatism's discussions of reference provide an adequate terminology for our analysis. Now that we know that the deconstructive possibility haunts all attempts at system-building, it is time to engage in a new kind of dialogue with the referential strategies of texts. That is, we need to resituate the problem of reference within a post-structuralist horizon, so that we can reopen the questions of linguistic representation in the works of these authors.

The landmark study of reference is Gottlob Frege's "Sense and Reference,"[9] in which the author distinguishes among three levels in linguistic expressions: the level of subjective, psychological consciousness that includes private associations, or "Ideas" [*Vorstellungen*]; the level of public, objective meaning or "sense"; and the level of reference. Frege excludes the first level from analysis and shows how the separation of sense and reference explains the possibility that two concepts may designate the same referent. While the referent of a word is an object, the referent of an indicative sentence is its truth-value. Frege's theory, which is designed to produce logical and scientific truth, is precisely the kind of foundationalist correspondence theory of language that Rorty and Derrida have exploded.[10] Thus, even though Frege's distinctions are crucial for discussing the relationship of language and the "world," we need to rework his theory of sense by looking at Ferdinand de Saussure's theory.

Since Saussure completely avoids the problem of reference, his theory of the sign is much narrower than that of Frege. However, Saussure articulates the dynamics of meaning, an area that Frege's logical theory neglects. Saussure divides the linguistic sign into signifier (acoustic image) and signified (concept) and places signs in a linguistic system (*la langue*). Signs are defined by their relation to other members of the system—that is, their identity is relational, differential. This system is a synchronic state of language, a state that brackets language's historical (diachronic) changes, reference to the world, and individual speech-acts—*la parole*.

Emile Benveniste criticizes and reworks Saussure's analysis by distinguishing between the semiotic level of the sign, the exclusively intralinguistic relation that is Saussure's concern, and the semantic level of discourse, which operates at the level of the sentence and which includes the speech-acts of the subject in the world.[11] Hence, instead of a semiotic system, we have a semantic system, or what I shall call a system of social practices. These practices become the new structure, "ideality," or competence necessary to understand the event of the sentence or the text.[12] However, unlike the ideal meanings of Frege or Husserl, the space of social practices is not closed, homogeneous, and transparent to the subject, but traversed by aesthetic, political, and linguistic forces. The subject is not bracketed out of the system (Frege, Saussure) nor is he the ground for a theory of meaning (Husserl); instead, the subject and the world emerge through these practices.[13] This approach avoids the dangers of semiology that Derrida notes: "Communication presupposes subjects (whose identity and presence are constituted before the signifying operation) and objects (signified concepts, thought meaning that the passage of communication will have neither to constitute, nor by all rights, to transform). A communicates B to C" (*Positions*, 23). In the account that I am giving, reference to the subject or the world carries the potential to rupture the system—e.g., metaphor—and to release the system's potential for dissemination. Paul Ricoeur describes the linguistic and referential dynamism that emerges: "We master meaning by varying the conditions for use in relation to different referents. Conversely, we investigate new referents only by describing them as precisely as possible. Thus the referential field can extend beyond visible, perceptible things."[14] If language is not simply the tool of the subject who uses it to locate substances and ground epistemology, neither is it merely a chain of signifiers. Language is the medium within which we live, a medium with the ontological power that, as Martin Heidegger says, can cover over and disclose a "world(s)."[15]

To this point, we have discussed reference only at the level of the sentence, not at the level of the text. Edouard Morot-Sir extends the theory of reference to the text: "Every text is the result of two combined forces—the referential force and the argumentative force, which are complementary aspects of what is known as illocutionary force. The text is thus the result of a double anchoring—the extralinguistic anchor of reference and the intralinguistic anchor of argumentation."[16] Reference is not a way of hooking language onto objects but a force and a value that emerges in and through the text. These forces help the text to carve out its own semantic space with regard to the tradition—that is, each text articulates itself within a field of intertextuality. Hence, this post-structuralist problematic of reference will help us reveal the strategies through which texts generate their own ontologies, their own "worlds." "Worlds" is obviously a metaphor, which has been developed by Nelson Goodman in *The Ways of World Making*,[17] and the reader may find this metaphor to be an overly melodramatic way of discussing differences among and within texts. Rorty, for instance, criticizes Goodman's trope and claims that "we need not go beyond the more straightforward 'many descriptions of the same world' (provided one does not ask, 'And what world is that?')" (*Consequences*, xlvii). Since this is precisely the question that I want to raise, we are left with the metaphor. Moreover, the notion of world will help foreground the ontological dimension of the texts neglected by traditional treatments of realism, the way (in Heidegger's phrase) "Being speaks always and everywhere throughout language."[18]

The problematic I have just sketched will provide the touchstone for discussing the referential strategies of three great novelists in the realistic tradition of the nineteenth and early twentieth centuries, Balzac, Flaubert, and James. Because the value of my approach emerges through close analysis of individual texts, I have selected one novel by each author: *Les Illusions perdues* (1843), *L'Education sentimentale* (1869), and *The Golden Bowl* (1904).[19] These widely known texts recommend themselves for several reasons. First, they represent important and historically distinct variations on the ubiquitous, nineteenth-century type, the *Bildungsroman*,[20] in which a young character is initiated into the complexities of society. Such a structure provides an opportunity to examine the relationship between realism and knowledge, since the protagonist's understanding, not just his actions, is foregrounded. Second, these novels illustrate three different uses of history and setting, which are closely associated with realism.

Realism is a notoriously slippery term that has been used in so many contexts that its meaning threatens to disappear. Since this study is concerned with the problem of language and reference, we can omit definitions that focus on the objects of representation, such as Erich Auerbach's.[21] Those definitions that do address the question of representation characteristically exile the question of language. *The Encyclopedia of Philosophy* calls realism "the view that material objects exist externally to us and independently of our sense experience."[22] In *On Realism*, J. P. Stern offers a formula that is filled with terms that contemporary criticism puts into question (facts, the ocular metaphor, the position of the subject): "Realism [of all periods] is no more, and no less, than an undertaking to look all the relevant facts in the face."[23] George Levine's interesting recent study *The Realistic Imagination* clearly articulates the assumptions of the realistic project for our purposes. First, he opposes language and realism. The realistic author seeks "to avoid the conventionality of language in pursuit of the unattainable unmediated reality. Hence, realism is a "self-conscious *effort* . . . to make literature appear to be describing directly not some other language but reality itself (whatever that may mean)."[24] He goes on to say that the "epistemology that lay behind realism was empiricist, with a tendency to value immediate experience over continuities or systems of order . . ." (18). In all of these definitions we see realism and reference bound together into a cluster of mutually reinforcing terms: perception, empiricism, epistemology, and psychology of the subject. Realistic ontology is an ontology of substances that exiles the question of language. These presuppositions produce a reading that illustrates how Flaubert and James represent stylistic and psychological refinements of Balzacian realism while remaining true to Balzac's realistic paradigm.[25] In this reading, the use of point of view in Flaubert and James does not challenge the epistemological, perceptual ground of realism but reinforces it.[26] Moreover, what informs most readings is the identification of reference and realism, which in turn becomes a defense of representationalism. Thus, Levine poses his book as "a challenge to the antireferential bias of our criticism and to the method of radical deconstruction" (3). The present study will define realism in terms of linguistic strategies and make these strategies only one kind of referential possibility, so that we can open up the ways the language of the texts evokes their worlds.

I shall consider realism to be a set of discourse strategies that encourage the reader to believe in the text's referential power, not an imitation of the external world. In "Un Discours contraint," Philippe Hamon outlines the presuppositions of realistic discourse in terms that are compatible with the theory of reference:

1. The world is rich, diverse ... discontinuous;
2. I can transmit information about this world;
3. Language can copy the world;
4. Language is secondary to the real (it expresses the real but does not create the real; it is "exterior" to the real);
5. The words of the message must be as transparent as possible;
6. The enunciation of the message (style) must be effaced as much as possible;
7. The reader must believe in the truth of my information about the world.[27]

The realistic system thus presumes that the speaker (or writer), the listener (reader), and others are all joined by conventions of verisimilitude and englobed in an ontologically unified world. This unity is produced by a hierarchy of discourses that fix the relationship of signifier and signified between concepts and referents. This system faces three kinds of threats to its control of representation: fluidity at the level of meaning (e.g., puns, metaphors); reference to entities that are outside the existing categories for naming the world (e.g., through neologisms, abstractions [a Jamesian favorite], or indexicals such as "I" or "this"); reference to the system itself (e.g., metalanguage such as, "We've been speaking in realistic discourse; let's not").

In the course of the first three chapters, I shall develop the nature of realistic discourse by using Balzac's *Les Illusions perdues* as a source for these strategies; however, I shall not give a reading of the novel or probe for its discontinuities.[28] (There are no chapters devoted exclusively to Balzac's novel.) Instead, this text will provide a background throughout the analysis of *L'Education sentimentale* and *The Golden Bowl*. In Balzac, the real does not threaten the ontological integrity of the knower or the known; and the known, which is a semantic system of meanings and referents, links the reader, the narrator, and the informed characters, the so-called initiators of the *Bildungsroman*. What Balzac's Lucien de Rubempré must learn is articulated by others. Flaubert's Frédéric Moreau and James's Maggie Verver do not evolve toward a fixed knowledge. Rather, the characters (and the reader) are exposed to the fluidity of sense and reference. The difficulty of saying what something is, of bringing sense and reference together into a system of knowledge is dramatized in different ways by *L'Education* and *The Golden Bowl* and my analysis of each novel is organized around four problems of the realistic novel:

1. The creation of physical and cultural space;
2. The speech of the characters and the relationship of their speech to what the text suggests knowledge to be;
3. The narrator's authority and his interventions;
4. The representation of the protagonist's experience.

Thus, the structure of my exposition is both parallel and progressive. It is parallel in that I consider the same set of problems for each novel; it is progressive in that I show how Flaubert's novel explodes the presuppositions of Balzacian realism and how in *The Golden Bowl* the system of realism is only one of the systems to which characters refer.

Since my critical approach differs markedly from those of other critics, my dialogue with them will be limited. In the first half of my study, I discuss the principal commentaries on *L'Education* and show how these readings differ from my own. However, the section on James builds on the preceding argument and hence does not repeat my case against reading strategies that I have already discussed. The only work that I analyze at any length is Ruth Bernard Yeazell's *Language and Knowledge in the Late Novels of Henry James*. Her excellent book, which opens a new pathway into the mysteries of Jamesian language, treats many of the issues that I do, and my debates with her are arguments against her presuppositions more than against her readings. Since her presuppositions are widely shared, even by those who disagree with her, I have not made specific reference to the enormous number of interpretations of the novel.

The purpose of this study is not simply to offer another reading of these texts but to provide a new way of looking at the development of the novel that focuses on referential strategies rather than objects of representation. A recent approach to these authors has been to link James and Balzac and to exile Flaubert, as in Peter Brooks's *The Melodramatic Imagination: Balzac, Henry James, Melodrama and the Mode of Excess* and William Stowe's *Balzac, Henry James and the Realistic Novel*. Brooks says, "Meaning, he [Flaubert] implies, cannot be manufactured in the Balzacian manner. From a search for the hidden signified and its metaphorical absent presence we are led rather to a play of the signifier: the reader's engagement with the plane of representation as pure surface and with the process of narration.... The counter-tradition of Flaubert stands in contrast to the expressionism of Balzac and James" (198–99). Although Stowe does not use Saussurian theory (signifier/signified), as does Brooks, the purpose of his book is not to provide a new definition of realism or to examine the linguistic drama of texts but to bridge the gap he sees in current criticism between "textuality" and "faithfulness to observed reality" (173). By starting with a post-structuralist theory of reference, my study situates our critical discussion beyond this opposition between the "radical" defenders of textualism and the "old-fashioned" adherents of representation and brings these three authors into a new dialogue with each other and the question of realism.[29]

The most interesting commentator on Balzac and Flaubert is James himself, who was introduced to Flaubert in 1876 by Turgenev and who wrote four essays on Flaubert and five on Balzac. Since James's literary criticism has been read as a source for New Criticism and Formalism as well as for realism, I shall not enter into the lengthy reinterpretation that the use of his essays would require.[30] Nonetheless, his remarks on Flaubert's novels raise important differences between *L'Education* and *The Golden Bowl* and suggest the nature of the relationship that I want to establish. James's objections cluster around two points: Flaubert's novels are concerned primarily with the language of perception, and the consciousness of the central characters is too limited.

> M. Flaubert's theory as a novelist, briefly expressed, is to begin on the outside. Human life, we may imagine his saying, is before all things a spectacle, an occupation and entertainment for the eyes. What our eyes show us is all that we are sure of. ("Charles de Bernard and Gustave Flaubert" [1876])
>
> No one will care for him at all who does not care for his metaphors, and those moreover who care most for these will be discreet enough to admit that even a style rich in similes is limited when it renders only the visible. The invisible Flaubert scarcely touches; his vocabulary and all his methods were alien to it.... He had no faith in the power of his moral to offer a surface. ("Gustave Flaubert" [1893])
>
> Why did Flaubert choose, as special conduits of the life he proposed to depict, such inferior and in the case of Frédéric such abject human specimens?[31] ("Gustave Flaubert" [1902])

James's remarks point to some undeniable features of Flaubert's text. *L'Education* is, for the most part, restricted to the language of perception, even if this language sometimes appears in a reverie. Moreover, from the point of view of the Jamesian novel, Frédéric's consciousness offers little depth. By contrast, *The Golden Bowl* represents a world filled with invisible referents generated by minds and languages that are not constrained by positivistic discourse. However, these differences do not sever crucial connections between Flaubert and James. *L'Education* is not a realistic novel in the Balzacian sense, for it irrealizes the realistic discourse of *Les Illusions perdues*. Sense and reference do not cohere to form a kind of knowledge that the character masters, as in Balzac's novel. Rather, Frédéric's consciousness is at the mercy of a language that is not a spiritual instrument but an opaque and recalcitrant object. What communication or accomplishments there are in the novel are devalued. The text is inhabited by an evil that infects the language of representation, not just Frédéric's mind. The hero frequently falls through the thin membrane of identity, outside the received meanings and referents, outside the ontology of realism. This ontological discontinuity is the link between *L'Education sentimentale* and *The Golden Bowl*, and what distinguishes them from *Les Illusions perdues*.

Part One
Balzac and Flaubert

1
Setting: Reference Beyond Signification

THE setting of *L'Education sentimentale* has all the features of the realistic novel. It is set in a historical place (Paris), in a defined historical period (1840–51, with an epilogue in 1867), and there are many details about the social environment without the suggestion of a transcendent realm beyond the positivistic world of sensations and facts. For the most part, the narrator generates the setting without reference to the narrative instance (e.g., use of first or second person or adverbs that refer to time of narration) and thus emphasizes the forces of disengagement, of reference.[1] Neither the sense nor the reference of the words seems problematic. The text's setting could therefore be read as simply a refined version of the representation of Parisian society in *Les Illusions perdues*, a representation that is purged of needless commentary and metaphoric extravagance in Balzac's text.

Nonetheless, this apparently unproblematic setting has been read in a variety of ways, and the center of the controversy is description. For Flaubert's contemporaries, the text's description violates the norms of the novel. Barbey d'Aurevilly says, "This novel's style is description, an infinite, eternal, atomistic and blind description that takes up the entire book and replaces all the faculties of the mind."[2] Indeed, these early critics find that the novel breaks almost all textual norms of the day. René Dumesnil summarizes their reaction:

"The same complaints, the same arguments are repeated from one article to the next as if all the critics had agreed about what they were going to say and decided to crush Flaubert under the weight of their censure" (178). Though I cannot go into the fascinating reception of the text, a brief look at two opposing modern traditions of reading will help to locate my own analysis on the map of criticism and to clear a path for the discussion in the succeeding chapters.

One of the traditions reads the description according to realistic and New Critical criteria (e.g., Victor Brombert and Robert Sherrington); another tradition, the structuralist readings of Jonathan Culler and Roland Barthes, finds that the text explodes the institution of the realistic novel.³ The issue revolves on whether some of the novel's descriptions are gratuitous. The New Critical reading recuperates all descriptions by assigning them to a function—e.g., they reveal the psychology of the character who views them—or by finding thematic analogies that unify the work. The other tradition maintains that some descriptions cannot be recuperated into the literary tradition and that the text thus breaks with the institution of the novel. "Recuperability" joins the question of reference since understanding reference depends on the discourse situation, the speaker and the context. If these factors become ambiguous, then the referential effect will change. Since my reading follows Culler's to a certain extent, I shall begin with an example that violates the discourse of realism. The following description appears in Part II when Frédéric returns to Paris after his inheritance:

> The plain had changed beyond recognition and looked like a town in ruins. The fortifications crossed it in a horizontal ridge, and on the unpaved paths edging the road stood small branchless trees protected by battens bristling with nails. Chemical factories alternated with timber-merchants' yards. Tall gateways, like those of farms, revealed between their half-open doors sordid yards full of refuse, with pools of dirty water in the middle. Long-fronted, dull red taverns displayed a pair of crossed billiard cues in a wreath of painted flowers between their first-floor windows; here and there a little stucco shanty had been left half-finished. (102; 110)

The most important feature of the passage is that the language of representation is the language of perception, not whether the description is reported from the narrator's or Frédéric's point of view. (The scene opens a new paragraph, and the last sentence of the preceding paragraph includes a perceptual verb: "all of a sudden he caught sight of the dome of the Pantheon.") The passage does not seem to emphasize a thematic point nor insert itself into plot-functions (e.g., expositions) or character-functions. One could index these details with a category such as "the horror of industrialization," but this category does not account for the passage's independence from literary functions or from social purposes in the represented world. The referential power of the language gives the objects a hallucinatory quality, as if they were contemplated without regard to their practical uses, as if matter were asserting its autonomy from humanity. The eye of observation does not master reference.

This autonomy of the representation of objects is even more striking in the description of interior social settings than of the external environment. In the former, the reader expects not only the articulation of physical space but also of thematic space through redundancy or a general comment. The reader can accept purposelessness in natural objects more easily than in cultural artifacts supposedly informed by human intentions. In *L'Education* objects appear that can be grouped thematically—e.g., "eroticism," "bourgeois tastelessness"—however, the heterogeneity and the quantity of the objects overwhelm these thematic categories and the characters. A good example of this kind of description appears in Frédéric's introduction to Rosanette's salon at the beginning of Part II. This scene is typical of the *Bildungsroman*: the young provincial confronts a world that he does not understand but that the reader comprehends through his (the reader's) cultural knowledge, through the redundancy or symbolism of the description, through dialogue, or through the explanations of the narrator or initiator. In *Les Illusions perdues*, for example, Balzac's narrator sets up Lucien de Rubempré's first evening out in Paris as follows: "It was a memorable evening for him, thanks to his unvoiced repudiation of a great number of his ideas about life in the provinces. His little world was broadening out and society was assuming vaster proportions. The proximity of several beautiful Parisian women, so elegantly and so daintily attired, made him aware that Madame de Bargeton's *toilette*, though passably ambitious, was behind the times" (178; 161).[4] In the scene at Rosanette's, however, there is no explanatory dialogue, little reflection by the hero, and almost no action. Balzacian description is inserted into the plot so that the objects participate in the action even if they do not assume an actantial function themselves. Objects are not just phenomena but actors whose meaning emerges through their history. Since action and social discourse in *L'Educa-*

tion are displaced by description—with regard to Balzacian text—what is traditionally "background" takes on a great semantic burden. (The scene occupies fifteen pages.) The following passage appears at its beginning:

> At first Frédéric was dazzled by the lights; he could see nothing but silk, velvet, bare shoulders, a mass of colours swaying to the strains of an orchestra hidden by some foliage, between walls hung with yellow silk, and adorned here and there with pastel portraits and crystal sconces in the Louis Seize style. Tall lamps, whose frosted globes looked like snowballs, rose above baskets of flowers which stood on little tables in the corners; and opposite, beyond a second smaller room, a third could be seen, containing a bed with twisted posts and a Venetian mirror behind it. (114–15; 121–22)

Victor Brombert's reading of the scene illustrates how the passage can be integrated with other elements of the text and how Flaubert's differences from Balzac can be naturalized. First, Brombert compares the scene with the Taillefer orgy in *La Peau de chagrin* and dismisses the flatness of the description in *L'Education* by praising Flaubert. The critic finds "the same display of available carnality, the same specter of disease and death, the same garish couplings of the lascivious and the macabre. Only Flaubert is not concerned with sheer pyrotechnics" (130). Finding a unifying bordello motif, he then relates this scene to one at Dambreuse's and to one at the café Alhambra. Brombert sees the menacing heterogeneity of the objects in the last of these scenes; however, he naturalizes heterogeneity by making the bordello motif a metaphor: "This shocking combination is not merely a sign of vulgarity. It represents the particular attempt at facile poetry.... In this light, the bordello becomes the convenient metaphor for any catering to the thirst for illusion." Invested with the power of metaphor, the bordello gathers fragmented meanings and unifies the text: "This aspect of the metaphorical unity of *L'Education sentimentale* is further strengthened by the presence of key characters who, in one form or another, are for sale" (131).

Culler shows how the description in the scene at Rosanette's resists Brombert's thematic and symbolic recuperation, and his discussion is worth summarizing here. He supports his contention by following Brombert's suggestion and comparing the description in *La Peau de chagrin* with that in *L'Education*. Even though both passages include many similar objects, they are not presented in the same way. Balzac's objects are framed by an englobing proposition that links the objects to human interests and makes them illustrations of this interest: "The whole company remained for a moment immobile and charmed on the threshold. The excessive pleasures of the feast paled before the tempting spectacle that the host offered to the most voluptuous of their senses" (Culler, 94). Diversity in the scene is contained by the sentence that generalizes the force of the objects and associates them with known desires: "This harem offered visual seductions, voluptuous pleasures for all caprices" (Culler, 96). These suggestions for reading the objects are reinforced by what Culler calls "synoptic movements," a panorama that contains the scene visually and semantically: "The salons at this moment presented an advance view of Milton's Pandemonium" (Culler, 99). In the passage from *L'Education*, the objects are not offered as knowledge. Frédéric perceives these objects, but perception of their existence is not followed by synthetic statements about the meaning of these objects nor is the reader given clues that escape Frédéric. Here and elsewhere in the novel, the hero's response is stunned silence or a reverie that is independent of the objects that stimulate it. Balzac's text moves easily between the language of designation and the language of explanation so that the milieu, the individual characters, and the society are interconnected. Balzac's narrator often makes those connections allegorical as well as causal. In *Les Illusions perdues*, we read: "The outside of the Séchard premises was in keeping with the squalor reigning inside" (58; 25). After a description of Lousteau's room, the narrator says: "This room, at once dirty and dreary, gave evidence of a life lacking both repose and dignity" (258; 253). Objects in the text are always placed in systems of signification that act on the characters, and the narrator of *Les Illusions* makes explicit what is implicit in most realistic novels: "It is all the more necessary at this point to make some remarks on Angouleme because they will help us to understand Madame de Bargeton, one of the most important characters of this story" (64; 31).

To this point, my analysis is consistent with Culler's; I disagree, however, with the limits imposed by his conclusion that we should read for "the ways in which . . . it is written against the novel as institution" (109). Culler's analysis is thus intended not only to show the difference between Balzac's text and Flaubert's but to show how *L'Education* resists all attempts to read it. This attempt differs from my reading in several ways. First, it equates the Balzacian novel with the "institution of the novel"—with the reader's intertexts in the genre. Second, it makes no distinction between the interpretative strategy and the text. For Culler, texts are either intelligible or unintelligible, recuperable or nonrecuperable. That is, texts and commentary "fit" in recuperable texts, while unreadable texts are not appropriate for commentary. In brief, he uses a structuralist model of genre in which Balzac's texts are the norm. My reading invokes modern intertexts (specifically Beckett), rejects the opposition intelligible/unintelligible for Balzac and Flaubert and attempts to separate text and reading, though such a separation is not "objective" but defined by my own hermeneutic position that sets up a dialogue between "text" and critical language. The difference between Balzac and Flaubert's texts does not mean that all interpretations are inappropriate except the antinovelistic one; nor does it mean that reference must serve the interests of realism. Instead, *L'Education* opens possibilities at the same time that it questions the presuppositions of Balzacian realism. An examination of Roland Barthes's important article "L'Effet de réel"[5] will show how this possibility is opened.

In this article Barthes examines a short description from "Un Coeur simple" and assigns those details that do not have a thematic function to a new function that he calls "the real," a category that appears in the nineteenth century.[6] The innovative nature of this feature of the novel can be seen in the comments of Balzac's narrator who wants to assure the reader that the details in his work are both real and necessary to the story. After Balzac, the "real" entered into the system of verisimilitude that is available to the reader and the justification for such "superfluous" material was no longer necessary. In most novels during this period "the real" is just such an innocuous category that does not raise the problematic nature of the representation nor the relationship of the characters to these objects. The description in *L'Education*, however, breaks this category by overloading it with objects that hover outside the discourse of the characters.

Flaubert's text thus brings into conflict two models of understanding that dominate the nineteenth century—observation and narrative. In "Narrate or Describe?"[7] Georg Lukács condemns Flaubert and Zola for replacing narration with description so that objects do not become part of the actions of the characters, as in Balzac and Tolstoy: "The description of things no longer has anything to do with the lives of the characters" (132). The result is that "description merely levels" (127) and "contemporizes everything," whereas "narration recounts the past" (130). Although I do not follow Lukács's call for a centered narrative, his analysis brings Flaubert's text to crisis. That is, by interrogating the text in terms of narrative, Lukács asks us to consider the way the text's description presents unrepresentable social and economic forces through these objects, objects that cannot be represented in narrative. Listing objects calls up their tangled histories and opens a fissure between observation and mastery. However, the importance of this fissure cannot be reduced to the modernist reading, in which Flaubert violates the generic patterns of the classic realist text. Rather, the text's description—as well as other features—also makes the novel available to a postmodern reading, in which representability and narration are thematized.[8]

The simple naming of objects in the language of perception is called into question. In these evocations of matter, the reference to things opens a hole in signification. Barthes describes this power of reference: "The best way for a language to be indirect is to refer as constantly as possible to objects and not to their concepts."[9] In these passages the language of perception is not just relativized through the point of view, but is given an ontological force that overwhelms the characters and their language.[10] In his essay "Wittgenstein's Problem," Maurice Blanchot discusses Flaubert's struggle with language, with "l'Autre de la parole":

> Now, ever since Mallarmé we have felt that the other of language is always posed by the language itself as that in which it looks for a way out, in order to disappear into it, or for an Outside, in which to be reflected. Which means not simply that the Other is already part of *this* language, but that as soon as this language turns around to respond to its Other, it is turning towards another language, and we must be aware that this other language is other, and also that it, too, has its Other. At this point we come very close to Wittgenstein's problem, as corrected by Bertrand Russell: that every language has a structure about which one can say nothing *in* that language, but that there must be another language dealing with the structure of the first and possessing a new structure about which one cannot say anything except in a third language—and so forth. Several consequences follow from this, among them these: 1) what is inexpressible is inexpressible in relation to a certain system of expression; 2) although there may be reason to regard the group of things and values as constituting a whole (for example, in a given scientific conception . . .), the virtual group of the different possibilities of speech could not constitute a total-

ity; 3) the Other of all speech is never anything but the Other of a given speech or else the *infinite movement* through which one mode of expression—always prepared to extend itself in the multiple requirements of simultaneous series—fights itself, exalts itself, challenges itself or obliterates itself in some other mode.[11]

These evocations of things in *L'Education* do not indicate the triumph of the designative power of language to fix the world but the presence of the unknown in language, objects, and consciousness. Physical objects resemble the space of Beckett's plays (particularly *Krapp's Last Tape* and *Happy Days*), where the staging solicits and crushes human speech and desire.[12] Moreover, in Flaubert's text as in these plays, matter is not securely outside the subject; rather, it invades consciousness and speech.

The setting is not just composed of objects that are named by a subjectless text. It is also composed of historical names. The originality of the role of these names in *L'Education* emerges clearly against the use of these names in *Les Illusions perdues*. Historical names appear extensively in Balzac's novel, and they serve to link the narrator's discourse to the historical world outside. Authors' names are sometimes used in the narrator's address to the reader, in which reference to this common known entity helps the reader to understand the representation.[13] For example, in the description of Nicolas Séchard, we read: "His cranium, completely bald on top, though it was still fringed with greying curls, called to mind the Franciscan friars in La Fontaine's *Tales*" (42; 7). To help us grasp Lucien's disillusionment, the narrator invokes our knowledge of Rousseau and then secures the link between history, verisimilitude, and the text by asking us to assent to the probability and the naturalness of the feeling: "Losing his illusions about Madame de Bargeton while Madame de Bargeton was losing hers about him, the unhappy youth, whose destiny was a little like that of Jean-Jacques Rousseau, imitated him in this respect: he was fascinated by Madame d'Espard and fell in love with her immediately. Men who are young or who remember the emotions of their youth will understand that this passion was extremely likely and natural" (193; 178).

This kind of reference between narrator and reader, which almost never appears in *L'Education*, helps establish the appropriation of history by the text. The narrator speaks of historical figures in the same way as he does of characters. In addition, historical names play a prominent role in the story itself, both in the narrator's exposition and in the characters' own speech, not just in the extradiegetic language of the narrator. In the portrait of Meyraux, one of the members of the Cénacle, the narrator tells us that this character "died after initiating the famous discussion between Cuvier and Saint-Hilaire over a momentous question which was to divide the world of scientists into equal camps behind these two men of genius. He died some months before the former, who stood out for a narrow, analytical science as against the pantheistic Saint-Hilaire who is still alive and is revered in Germany" (227; 218). The narrator takes up historical authors and their ideas, masters them by his own language, and connects the time of their lives to the narrative instance. Moreover, the presence of historical authors is reinforced by their appearance in dialogue. Lucien and David discuss André Chénier and one of the lines that they read together appears in the text (61–62; 28–29). Daniel d'Arthez criticizes Lucien for his imitation of Walter Scott: "If you don't want to ape Walter Scott you must invent a different manner for yourself, whereas you have imitated him" (223; 213). Thus, when the narrator describes Mme de Bargeton's hazy uncritical reading of romantic authors, a background that resembles that of Frédéric or Emma Bovary, he (the narrator) also assures us of the system of the "real" that surrounds her infection with these authors: "She worshipped Lord Byron, Jean-Jacques Rousseau and those who led poetic and dramatic lives" (71–72; 41).

In *L'Education sentimentale* historical names do not participate in the creation of an authoritarian language that englobes the text and absorbs history. On the contrary, these names participate in irrealization of history. One of the ways that this process operates is through listing and intermingling of authors so that their specific ideas are not only never articulated but are designated by a language that makes no differences among them: "he [Frédéric] prized passion above all else; Werther, René, Franck, Lara, Lelia, and other less distinguished writers roused him to almost equal enthusiasm" (15; 27). (This is also the case in *Madame Bovary*, where Emma's dreams are a mixture of various sources.) In the fascinating portrait of Sénécal, we learn that "he was familiar with Mably, Morelly, Fourier, Saint-Simon, Comte, Cabet, Louis Blanc," but what appears in his speech is indistinct: "out of this mixture he had evolved an ideal of virtuous democracy..." (137; 141). In the dialogues, proper names are bandied about with little comprehension. At Frédéric's apartment, the talk turns to Malthus, but Cisy does not know who he is and the topic is dropped (138; 143). Of the conversation at the café Alhambra, we read the following narration: "an argument followed which touched on [*mêla*] Shakespeare, the censorship, style, the lower classes, the takings at the Porte-Saint-Martin, Alexandre Dumas, Victor Hugo, and Dumersan" (74; 83). (The French verb "mêler" indicates a confusion that Baldick's translation does not capture.) In all of these cases, historical names, like historical facts, are an eruption of the real in the text, and these allusions engage the reader's cultural knowledge only to dissipate the coherence of this knowledge in a cacophony of conflicting voices. The significations that these allusions bear are not ordered by an englobing voice as in *Les Illusions*. In Flaubert's text, historical allusions and objects are not part of a referentially secure discourse. The ideas that appear in the text do not "belong" to any authors, for these ideas are an anonymous melange of *lieux communs*. As Sartre says of Flaubert's *Dictionnaire des idées reçues:* "More than a thousand articles, and who feels attacked? No one."[14] History's power to guarantee meaning, to serve as a referent for fiction, is shaken and reinscribed, so that both are deconstructed. Derrida describes the deconstructive project as a challenge to our assumptions about the relationship between text and reference, not as an assertion of the autoreferentiality of all texts: "What is produced in the current trembling is a reevaluation of the relationship between the general text and what was believed to be, in the form of reality (history, politics, economics, sexuality, etc.), the simple referable exterior of language or writing . . ." (*Positions*, 91).

The style of *L'Education* is both limpid and opaque. The classic, heavy sentence-structure and diction homogenizes description, speech, and narration, a style that Proust calls "un trottoir roulant." In his brilliant article "A propos du style de Flaubert,"[15] Proust describes how Flaubert's style asserts its singularity and unity ("l'hermétique continuité du style" [74]), at the same time that it spreads itself over a reality swarming with different objects and languages, "those heavy materials that the Flaubertian sentence raises and drops again with the intermittent noise of an excavator" (83). This extraordinary setting conditions the characters' speech, the subject of the next chapter.

2
Speech and Knowledge: Language Without Subjects

> La bêtise n'est pas d'un côté et l'esprit de l'autre. C'est comme le vice et la vertu. Malin qui les distingue. Axiome: le synthétisme et la grande loi de l'ontologie.
> —Gustave Flaubert

> Idle talk is the possibility of understanding everything without previously making the thing one's own.[1]
> —Martin Heidegger

THE relationship of speech and knowledge is crucial to the *Bildungsroman* (and realism), and it is one of the presuppositions of representation that *L'Education* rewrites. In the traditional *Bildungsroman*, such as *Les Illusions perdues*, the hero acquires his knowledge from dialogues with the experienced characters, and the most important indication that the hero has learned something is his ability to speak the language of society—i.e., to interact successfully—and to make statements about the nature of society. For example, when Lucien comes to Paris and meets Daniel d'Arthez, the ethically pure artist, the latter explains the traps that society leaves for young authors (220–25; 209–15). Etienne Lousteau, a writer who has been seduced by the glitter of commercialism, initiates Lucien into journalism (250–57; 244–52). Even though Etienne is primarily an apologist for the social system who delights in revealing Lucien's illusions, the forces that he describes coincide with those depicted by Daniel.[2] These two characters establish the opposition between Lucien's desire for artistic development and his ambition. That is, the statements of the speakers have the same referential power. They prove to be accurate predictions, and they are in accord with the narrator's judgment. After one of Lousteau's speeches, the narrator describes the effect on the hero and endorses Lousteau's representation: "Lucien was stupefied as he listened to Lousteau's words: the scales fell from his eyes and he became alive to literary truths of which he had not even guessed" (348; 358). The statements of both Daniel and Etienne subscribe to the same ontology as does the narrator, though the two initiators have opposing moral positions. Moreover, the acts of enunciation are not problematic. These initiators or Lucien may make errors, speak irrationally, or reveal more than they are conscious of, but their speech-acts never make the reader question the subject's mastery of meaning. Lucien is able to take up the knowledge offered by his friends and articulate the opposition between moral and economic forces:

> The more the Cénacle tried to turn Lucien away from this path, the more did his desire to brave the peril invite him to take the risk. He began to argue with himself: was it not ridiculous to let himself be once more overtaken by penury without doing anything to avert it? In view of the failure he had met with regard to his first novel, Lucien felt little inclined to settle down to a second one. Besides, what would he have to live on while he was writing it? (237; 229)

Lucien thus learns the terms of the opposition and continues these interior reflections during his increasing involvement with journalism and society. (See 320, 326, for another of the hero's reflections.) The language of the characters, the narrator, and the reader are bound together by *clichés* and *lieux communs*.[3] As Ruth Amossy says of the *cliché* in Balzac:

> Clichés assure a smooth transition from the character of the story to fictive public opinion and to the presupposed belief that the narrator and the reader share. In precisely this way, they "naturalize" fiction and make its meaning transparent. The use of the cliché thus tends first to guarantee the transitivity of the realistic text, to insert it, if not in a real world, at least in a pre-existing discursive network. (54–55)[4]

However, the character's development is not just an acquisition of information but a reconstitution of himself. In Angoulême, Lucien sees Mme de Bargeton as an enchanting mistress and himself as a Romantic poet. In Paris, he finds that his mistress loses her glimmer and that his conception of himself is considered ridiculous. Such a transformation suggests perspectivism and cultural relativism, which is often used to define "modernism" in Flaubert,

James, and Balzac; but this designation obscures important differences among their texts. Martin Kanes in his *Balzac and the Comedy of Words* tries to establish Balzac's epistemological modernity in just this way. Kanes maintains that the placement of the characters in different milieux illustrates Balzac's theory of language: "Only by subjecting his characters to radical shifts in milieu could the narrator show how the structure of reality is rooted in language and perception."⁵ "Whether Louise and Lucien are charming lovers or gawky country bumpkins, or a combination of both, depends almost entirely upon the progression of local perceptions and contexts; that is, upon comparisons" (237). However, the differences in the development of an individual character and among the various characters are mastered by the language and knowledge of the narrator and of the informed characters. The characters "progress," gain access to the Parisian world, and differences among people and places can be named. In addition, such an approach locates the issue at the level of the isolated individual rather than at the level of language and ontology.

In *L'Education*, the characters and the narrator have no such mastery over language and knowledge, nor does speech function in the same way as in the Balzacian novel. In her study of dialogue in Flaubert, Claudine Gothot-Mersch notes that unlike Balzac's dialogue, that of Flaubert "is often not part of the action, or a prologue to action; nor is it a disguise for narration." Not only does the dialogue refuse to serve a function in the plot, it also refuses to develop the psychology of a character: "In his dialogue, Flaubert does not depict characters but more comprehensive entities, types."⁶ However, the representation of speech in *L'Education* cannot be reduced to its novelistic function. The text challenges the realistic assumptions of the speech-act, in which speakers have access to a transparent linguistic system that they use to make pertinent statements in defined contexts.⁷ Flaubert's text problematizes the utterance, the act of enunciation, the referential force, and the ontology of the represented world.

One of the most obvious ways that the text challenges the situation of realistic discourse is through the effacement of the speaker. When Frédéric goes to a party at the Dambreuse's, we see the hero in a new setting that gathers together the political and economic representatives of society, that offers a *Bildungsroman* the opportunity to establish the forces of the text. Instead, we see language disembodied of a speaker:

Frédéric heard snatches of conversation such as these:
"Were you at the last charity ball at the Hotel Lambert, Mademoiselle?"
"No, Monsieur."
"It's going to be terribly hot soon."
"Yes, absolutely stifling."
"Whom is this polka by?" (158; 162)

Other speech is marked simply by an indefinite article and a profession: "a landowner was saying," "a law official launched an attack on the scandals of the theatre" (159; 162–63).

When the talk turns to the social turmoil, the guests express their disapproval, but the reader finds no homogeneous forces. Society appears primarily as a linguistic phenomenon rather than as an economic force. Language does not articulate a pre-existing reality but appears to be strangely independent of speakers and referents. Society is a collection of *lieux communs.* Thus, when Frédéric presents himself at the Club de l'Intelligence (302–9; 300–307), we do not find political discussion or intrigue as we do in Balzac's Paris but screaming inarticulate voices that alternately interrupt each other. Language does not efface itself in projects, communication, or action but refuses integration.

One could read the treatment of dialogue as illustrating the egotism or self-interest of the characters or the theme of "incommunicability" as does Brombert. However, such a reading does not distinguish this theme in Balzac or other realists from this theme in Flaubert. *L'Education* not only carries the theme of incommunicability, it explodes the monadic, self-contained subject who carries this theme. To call Flaubert's characters "self-serving" or "egotistical" is to give them a power they do not have. In *Les Illusions perdues*, the theme of incommunicability works differently. For example, when Lucien reads his poetry at the salon of Mme de Bargeton, the narrator explains that the other guests do not understand poetry: "The unhappy poet was unaware that with the exception of Madame de Bargeton poetry was a closed book to the minds of everyone present" (110; 86). Nonetheless, the narrator assures us that poetic discourse is comprehensible under the right conditions: "If poetry, when read or when recited, is to be understood, devout attention must be paid to it" (111; 87).

The capacity of language to manifest and master differences emerges most clearly in the Cénacle:

> These nine persons composed a fraternity in which esteem and friendship kept the peace between the most conflicting ideas and doctrines. . . . They all argued without quarrelling. They were without vanity, having no other audience than their own group. They told one another about their work and consulted one another with the amiable good faith of youth. (228; 219)

> Equally noble-hearted and equally strong in their convictions, they could think what they liked and say what they liked in matters both intellectual and scientific. (230; 221)

In *L'Education*, the problems of speech do not just appear in dialogue but also in the narrator's representation of speech in summary and narration. At an earlier scene at the Dambreuse's, we read,

> Then they deplored the immorality of servants, in connexion with a theft committed by a valet; and after that, one item of gossip followed another. Old Madame de Sommery had a cold. . . . The pettiness of the conversation seemed to be emphasized by the luxury of the setting; although the subject-matter was not as stupid as the manner of its delivery, which was aimless, lifeless, and inconsequential. (130; 135)

The narrator also uses words, signifiers, as focal points for the story. In this example, "property" becomes at once a unifying signifier to which different groups ascribe a different meaning: "Now property was raised to the level of Religion and became indistinguishable from God" (297; 295). The narrator thus foregrounds the rhetorical effects of the representation. Declarations for the Republic also become agreements that mark difference more pointedly than do disagreements:[8]

> And she declared herself in favour of the Republic, a position which had already been taken up by His Grace the Archbishop of Paris, and which was to be adopted with remarkable alacrity by the Magistrature, the Council of State, the Institut, the Marshals of France, Changarnier, Monsieur de Falloux, all the Bonapartists, all the Legitimists, and a considerable number of Orleanists. (294; 293)

This repetition of the same declaration deprives the statement of its conventional signification and makes the reference problematic. The flag of France becomes another emblem of difference: "everybody paid lip-service to the tricolour, each party seeing only one colour in the flag—its own—and resolving to remove the other two as soon as it had the upper hand" (295; 293).[9]

Language is thus not powerless; however, it is not the instrument of the individual subject who uses it to determine meaning and reference. Language is a heterogeneous magma that flows through consciousness and society somewhat independently of the subjects and the external referents that are supposed to control it. Economic, social, or other extralinguistic forces are not so much absent from the novel as they are inarticulated. These forces hover menacingly behind the rhetoric that tries to name them.

A similar problem emerges in the intimate gatherings, such as Frédéric's house-warming (136–42; 141–47), where each character takes up his own interest. Unlike the preceding passage from the Dambreuse's party where statements appear without a speaker, here the speaker is clearly identified and the speech is not obviously incoherent or gratuitous. Indeed, the narrator participates in the speech of the characters through indirect and free indirect discourse. ('FID' will henceforth denote free indirect discourse.) The effect of such passages is to show the *lieux communs* in all their clarity, to problematize the act of enunciation, and to efface the spoken language. After the narration announces the subject of the conversation (the murders of Buzançais and the food crisis), we see the following representation of what Sénécal says:[10]

> None of this would have happened if agriculture were better protected, if everything were not abandoned to competition, to anarchy, to the deplorable theories of *laissez-faire* and noninterference. This was how the feudalism of money, which was far worse than the old feudalism, came into being! But let them beware! In the end the people would lose patience and might well avenge their sufferings on the capitalists, either by sanguinary proscriptions or by the looting of their houses. (138; 143)

Free indirect discourse displaces Sénécal's voice as well as the narrator's. In direct speech subjectivity is questioned by its infection by *clichés* and *lieux communs* and by the way the speakers' words leap to their lips almost independently of the preceding statement. In free indirect representation, the power of the discourse to organize itself without mediation by the speaker is foregrounded even further.[11] Moreover, the dialogue in which this passage appears is directed at a particular historical incident; yet the dialogue does not develop the uniqueness of the incidents. Particular subjects become the occasion for representative, "typical" language that is deprived of a goal in the text. These topics are not developed by the plot or the character. Hence, the reader is invited to consider speech ahistorically and generally. This reading is further suggested by the text's refusal to employ colloquial speech, so that the diction of the dialogues and of narration are homogeneous, while the meaning, reference, and illocutionary forces are polyvalent.[12]

Not surprisingly, Sénécal, who is a revolutionary at the beginning of the novel, is swept along by the linguistic and extralinguistic currents. As the text unfolds, he adopts the language of the reactionaries and shoots the sympathetic Dussardier on the barricades (418; 411). The similarity of Sénécal's speech and public speech is emphasized in a paragraph of "idées régnantes" that Frédéric is trying to master in order to get a diplomatic position. The paragraph is in indirect and free indirect discourse. The heterogeneity of the voices behind "on" is the same heterogeneity behind Sénécal's own speech-acts:

> Some people wanted the Empire, some the Orleans family, some the Comte de Chambord; but all were agreed on the pressing need for decentralization. . . . [A]nd country life was praised to the skies, since illiterates were naturally more sensible than the rest of men. Hatred abounded: hatred of primary school teachers and wine-merchants, of philosophy classes and history lectures, of novels, red waistcoats, and long beards . . . ; for it was necessary to "restore the principle of authority." It did not matter in whose name it was wielded, or where it came from, provided it was strong and powerful. The Conservatives now talked like Sénécal. Frédéric no longer understood [ne comprenait plus]. (390; 385)

A common reading of the representation of speech is that Flaubert accurately (objectively) depicts his epoque, despite his pessimistic view of mankind. Sartre's brilliant study unmasks the New Critical identification of absence of commentary and objectivity. For Sartre, Flaubert's representation of speech reveals a theory of language founded on "la bêtise":

Thus stupidity [*la bêtise*] is infinite because it always comes from elsewhere—from another time, another place; it is inert and opaque, imposed by its weight, and its laws cannot be modified; it is a *thing*, finally, because it possesses the impassability and impenetrability of natural facts. The mechanical flattens against the living, generality suppresses the originality of singular experience, the prefabricated reaction is substituted for adapted praxis. This is the impersonal reign of the "One."[13]

Language is not the tool of the individual subject who manipulates it to his wishes, who uses it to represent what he sees or feels. The opposition between subject and object trembles. The subject is not an organizing intention but a logical space traversed by linguistic matter that is already formulated. (Cause-and-effect relations as well as symbolic relations are reduced to the arbitrary connections of the *idée reçue*.) Objects are not ontologically separate from "spiritual" subjects but invade this sanctum through the most insidious pathway, language.

However, the text does not just invite the reader to take an ironic, detached view of the representations; it demands his participation. This often occurs in the summarized, apparently naturalized dialogue, where the reader is asked to provide intertexts (literary or nonliterary) in order to understand the action. After Mme Arnoux confesses the burdens of her existence in a summarized paragraph of FID, we find the following one-sentence paragraph: "Frédéric declared that his life too was a failure" (171; 174). The reader must fill in the blank by referring himself to Balzac's *Le Lys dans la vallée*, where Félix de Vandenesse and Mme de Mortsauf exchange their similar sufferings. When Mme Arnoux encourages him to work and to marry, we do not find his words but a literary reference: "instead of giving the real reason of his despondency he invented another, nobler motive, posing as an ill-starred Antony—a language which was not entirely at variance with his ideas" (171; 174).

The text also invites the reader to consent to its causal or argumentative links between events (thoughts), links which are almost always asserted in FID. For example, after Frédéric reflects on the difficulty of telling Mme Arnoux of his love, we see the logical connections emerge in FID: "Besides (*d'ailleurs*), the children, the two maids, and the arrangement of the rooms raised insuperable difficulties. He therefore (*donc*) resolved to make her his alone and to go far away with her to live in some remote region" (171; 174–

75).¹⁴ Thus, even though the text diminishes the uniqueness of the individual's speech, it grants the subjectivity of the characters the power to constitute meanings and referents, the world. The narrator proposes no authoritarian language that "corrects" the representation by the voices of the characters as does the narrator of *Les Illusions perdues*.

The reader is also encouraged to consent to the "naturalness" of a topic of conversation or a sequence of events. In the following reported conversation, Dambreuse describes a possible position to Frédéric: "he [Frédéric] would find himself in daily contact with the most important men in Paris. As the Company's representative among the workers, he would naturally [*naturellement*] win their affection, and that would enable him later on to become a departmental councillor and then a deputy" (190; 193). In the text's summarized conversations the speech of the character is presented smoothly, chronologically, and the silences and awkwardness are eliminated.¹⁵ This same complicity is invited in the summary of the dialogue between Frédéric and Hussonet in Frédéric's apartment.

> They talked for hours, opening their hearts to one another. Hussonet hankered after the fame and profits of the theatre. He collaborated on musical comedies which were never produced, "had ideas galore" ["*avait des masses de plans*"], and wrote the words for songs: he sang one or two for Frédéric's benefit. Then, catching sight of a volume of Hugo and another of Lamartine in the bookcase, he launched out on to a sarcastic attack on the Romantic school. Those poets lacked common-sense and grammar, and above all they were not French! He prided himself on knowing his language and criticized the finest phrases with that cantankerous severity [*cette sévérité hargneuse*], that pedantic taste which characterizes frivolous-minded people when they come face to face with serious art. (33; 44)

Hussonet is the wittiest character in the novel, and the dialogue could be the satiric literary discussion that appears in Balzac's work. We discover his ambitions and his actions with one phrase of his speech ("*avait des masses de plans*") and another in FID. Then the narrator asks the reader to bring his knowledge to establish the way ("*avec cette sévérité hargneuse*") Hussonet criticizes the Romantics. Thus both Frédéric's romanticism and the ironic response to it are referred to as much as they are represented.

The reader is hence presented with homogeneous content and discontinuous discourse that assumes through a variety of voices that the reader already knows the story. Practical speech is presented either in scenes in which language is *déchaîné* or put in the background and reduced to an object by summary.

However, the conversations between Frédéric and Deslauriers and Frédéric and Mme Arnoux do not fit the foregoing analysis. In these dialogues, language functions as a stimulus to reveries and desires that are outside the socialized conventions. It often functions as a kind of prayer, where the goal is phatic more than communicative. Frédéric's relationships with these characters are not founded on *agape*, on shared sentiments and ideas. He is united with them by their capacity to stimulate very different dreams through their presence before each other and through the repetition of clichés. Frédéric's discussions with these characters often include mutual monologues where speech resembles a reverie that removes the characters from the spatial-temporal dimension of the novel and projects them into an alternative and emotionally fulfilling world. The form of these reveries is almost always a sequence of *lieux communs* and/or *clichés* that are represented indirectly and summarily rather than directly in the characters' own words. This pattern emerges in the expository flashback in I, 2, where the narrator summarizes iteratively both the topics and the successive steps in the conversations between the two friends, who are separated by "countless differences of character and breeding" (12; 25):

> They talked about what they would do later on, when they had left school. To begin with, they would go on a long voyage with the money Frédéric could deduct from his fortune when he came of age. Then they would come back to Paris and work together, never leaving each other; and as a relaxation from their labours, they would have love affairs with princesses in satin boudoirs, or wild orgies with famous courtesans. But doubts followed on their transports of hope. After fits of wordy gaiety they would relapse into profound silences. (13–14; 26)

Frédéric and Mme Arnoux have similar imaginative outpourings:

> And they imagined a life which would have been entirely devoted to love, rich enough to fill the widest deserts, surpassing all joys, and defying all sorrows; a life in which the hours

would have gone by in a continuous exchange of confidences; a life which would have become something splendid and sublime like the shimmering of the stars. (272; 271)

The typical reading of the preceding passages and the others like them is to say that the text (Flaubert) ironically exposes the romantic platitudes of his day and contrasts these pathetic dreams with the crass real world that surrounds and, indeed, inhabits the mediocre characters. However, if there is no ultimate language, the reader and the narrator are deprived of a space that can be juxtaposed to the discourse of the characters. Their stories and images are not to be condemned and ignored simply because they are clichés. These moments of reverie are the only places in the text where the characters escape the struggle of means and ends, a struggle that is undermined not so much by the characters' failures as by the futility of their successes. It is only at moments of reverie and silence that the characters open themselves to the ontological power of language. These reveries are projections into the past or future, projections that free images from concepts and that are neither rationalizations nor dreams. Gaston Bachelard describes the ontological power of reverie: "the being of the dreamer of the reverie is constituted by the images that this being solicits."[16] "The daydream assembles being around the day dreamer" (131). The reverie thus reveals possibilities outside of conceptual discourse: "The space in which the daydreamer is immersed is a plastic mediator between man and the universe. It seems that in the intermediary world where reality and reverie intermingle, a plasticity of man and his world is achieved in such a way that one never needs to know where the principle of this double malleability is" (144–45).

The most banal dialogues can be occasions where Frédéric feels an emotion that can solicit his imagination. In II, 6, Frédéric and Mme Arnoux meet by accident on the street and exchange pleasantries. At the end of their conversation, we learn that this superficial encounter gives him a space for rumination, even though these imaginings are not represented:

> The sunshine surrounded her; and her oval face, her long eyebrows, her black lace shawl moulding her shoulders, her dove-coloured shot-silk dress, the bunch of violets at one corner of her bonnet, all struck him as full of an extraordinary splendor. An infinite sweetness flowed from her lovely eyes;

and, stammering at random the first words which occurred to him, he said:
"How is Arnoux keeping?"
"Very well, thank you."
"And your children?"
"They are very well."
"Ah . . . ah . . . Lovely weather we're having, isn't it?"
"Yes, it's splendid."
"You're shopping?"
"Yes."
And with a slight inclination of her head she said:
"Good-bye."
She had not held out her hand to him, had not said a single affectionate word, had not even invited him to come and see her; but in spite of all that, he would not have exchanged this meeting for the most wonderful of adventures, and he savoured its sweetness [*il en ruminait la douceur*] as he continued on his way. (261; 260)

Thus if the text seems to bury its characters in codes and clichés that deprive these individuals of originality, it also exposes the failure of realism and positivism to link sense and reference in an ontologically certain world. *L'Education* irrealizes realistic speech and ontology. The powers and weaknesses of language to act independently of subjects and referents are foregrounded. However, the text's movement is not just critical, for it reveals the possibility that the novel can escape from positivism without returning to romanticism, that the language of the text can disclose a world and yet does not merely submit to the language of perception. Flaubert's text does not simply unmask society's stupidity but resituates the subject's relationship to language and the world. The "individual" is not a private personal space of uniqueness and "creativity." The characters and the narrator are always already embedded in social discourse, in what Heidegger calls "idle talk": "In it [idle talk], out of it, and against it, all genuine understanding, interpreting, and communicating, all re-discovering and appropriating anew, are performed" (*Being and Time*, 213). By resituating the subject within this space, the text not only shows the language's occlusive power but also its disclosive capacity. This is the opening that *The Golden Bowl* follows.

3
Narrator:
The Refusal of Authority

Un texte multivalent n'accomplit jusqu'au bout sa duplicité constitutive que s'il subvertit l'opposition du vrai et du faux, s'il n'attribue pas ses énoncés . . . à des autorités explicites, s'il déjoue tout respect de l'origine, de la paternité, de la propriété, s'il détruit la voix qui pourrait donner au texte son unité ('organique').
—Roland Barthes

La substance éthique du Réel est le Mal radical.[1]
—Jean-Paul Sartre

IF the speech of the characters provides no textual authority, then the reader looks to the narrator to provide him with an ultimate language. Indeed, this is where most critics find textual authority, though they often confound the narrator with Flaubert. In this view, Flaubert/narrator ironically exposes the foibles of his age and of human nature. The author/narrator thus controls the "showing," even though he generally refrains from "commentary." However, the narrator is not as stable as these critics would like. The narrator shifts perspectives, offers comments in different voices, disappears and invites the reader's sympathy and irony. Therefore, the force of the text's famous "impassibilité" cannot be reduced to the relative absence of commentary, to the opposition of showing/telling. The text is informed by powerful negative values, and at the same time the narrator refuses to take on the ordering authority of the traditional narrator of the *Bildungsroman*. Certainly, the narrator has the ostensible traits of omniscience, such as the ability to move freely through space and time and to represent characters' thoughts. He does not, however, offer the reader superior knowledge about the nature of the fictional world, establish a fixed authoritarian language, or incarnate himself. This absence of authority raises questions of ontology and value. The text does not "exemplify" the narrator's or the author's objective yet pessimistic representation of "the world" but renders the ontology of the representation problematic.

Le Mal that inhabits *L'Education* is in language and not just situated in a secure, monolithic, knowable reality.

The reader's difficulties with this unstable narrator can be seen in the commentary, which almost always appears in the portraits or in the narration of actions, not in the description of objects. In some of these remarks, the narrator adopts a social voice, the voice of the cliché, while other remarks seem to carry enough originality and insight to be taken seriously. The borderline between the maxim and the clichés is effaced, and the reader comes to suspect all formulated knowledge. For example, when Frédéric and Deslauriers get rid of Dussardier, the narrator remarks: "There are some men whose only function in life is to act as intermediaries; one crosses them as if they were bridges, and leaves them behind" (242). The comment has all the superficial glibness of Frédéric's own explanations, as we shall see. A remark on the hero's work on the history of the Renaissance is not so clearly marked: "He forgot his personality by immersing it in that of others—which is perhaps the only way to avoid suffering from it" (185; 188).[2]

The undecidability of these maxims recalls Flaubert's famous remark on a proposed preface to the *Dictionnaire des idées reçues:* "one would indicate [on indiquerait] how the work was intended to link the public to tradition, order, and social norms and would be organized in such a way that the reader couldn't tell if one was mocking him or not . . . [si on se fout de lui, oui ou non]."[3] Flaubert seems to anticipate Barthes's remark on voice that I cited in the epigraph. However, in his remark, Flaubert uses "on," instead of "je," to protect a site of writing that somehow escapes the positionality of all discourse. What is crucial for my reading is that this undecidability itself not become an insulated space where the author or the *scripteur* of the text can become a "malin génie" who plays just out of reach of the narratee. The sophisticated reader can then join the *scripteur* in the space of cosmic irony.[4]

Another ambiguous feature of the narrator's language is the recurrence of such phrases as "sans doute," "peut-être," "naturellement." (I exclude uses of "sans doute" that are in direct speech or free indirect speech of the characters or that are used to maintain focalization within Frédéric. For example, when Frédéric watches M. and Mme Arnoux, we read, "He [Arnoux] whispered something in her ear [Mme Arnoux's]—presumably a compliment, [une gracieuseté, sans doute], for she smiled" [6; 20].) In other places in the text, the narrator is responsible for the phrase. For example, in the portrait of Louise Roque: "C'était ces habitudes, sans doute, qui donnaient à sa figure une expression à la fois de hardiesse et de rêverie" (95) ("It was probably these games which lent to her face an expression at once bold and dreamy" [103]). The phrase also appears in the narrator's discussion of the hero's motives: "Elle lui sembla plus grande qu'à l'ordinaire, à cause de sa robe noire, sans doute" (99) ("She seemed taller than usual, probably because of her black dress" [107]); "Ce fut peut-être la pensée de Mme Arnoux qui le fit s'arrêter à l'étalage . . ." (113) ("It may have been the thought of Madame Arnoux which made him stop outside a secondhand dealer's shop . . . " [120]); "Frédéric s'excitait intérieurement à le mépriser encore plus, pour bannir, peut-être, l'espèce d'envie qu'il lui portait" (122) ("Frederic inwardly incited himself to despise him more than ever, possibly in order to banish a kind of envy which he felt for him" [122]). The effect of these phrases is to make the language used to represent the character's interior life a matter of speculation by a speaker and not constitutive of that life, as such language would be if it were spoken by an authoritarian narrator. Moreover, these speculations are usually conventional motives, arbitrary links between words and actions like the links between the words and the responses—they are not definitions—in *Le Dictionnaire des idées reçues*.

"Naturellement" also has the effect of calling the narrator's language into question. (I distinguish the appearance of this word in the narrator's speech from its appearance in the characters' thought or speech, which I examined in the last chapter.) For example, when Frédéric and Arnoux talk during their first meeting, we read, "La conversation roula d'abord sur les différentes espèces de tabacs, puis, tout naturellement, sur les femmes" (3). ("To begin with, the conversation touched on the different kinds of tobacco, and then turned quite naturally to women" [16].) (The *passé simple* assures the reader that this is the narrator's report and not FID.) When Rosanette is pursued by creditors, we read, "L'opposition à la saisie ayant été repoussée, la vente, naturellement, s'ensuivait" (396). ("The objection to the seizure having been overruled, the sale was automatically going to be held" [390].) At a dinner party chez Dambreuse, we read: "On arriva, tout naturellement, à relater différents traits de courage" (344). ("The guests were led very naturally to describe various feats of courage" [341].) In these cases, the reader is invited to see a link between the unfolding of events; however, the insistence of the "naturellement"calls attention to the arbitrariness and reversibility of the sequence. The seduction by *idées reçues* of narrative coherence and causality that afflict the characters' speech is alternately offered and denied by the narrator's speech. This instability works against *l'impassibilité* and the famous critical dictum from Flaubert's *Correspondance* that the author (narrator) should be like God in the universe, "présent partout et visible nulle part." My reading reverses the formula for the narrator's presence: "visible partout et présent nulle part."

Moreover, the authority of the narrator's language is challenged by the appearance of clichés. For example, in the portrait of Dambreuse, we read the following description: "et l'oreille dans tous les bureaux, la main dans toutes les entreprises, à l'affût des bonnes occasions, *subtil comme un Grec* et *laborieux comme un Auvergnat*, il avait amassé une fortune que l'on disait considérable" (19). ("with an ear in every office and finger in every pie, as wily as a Greek and as hard-working as an Auvergnat, he had amassed what was said to be a considerable fortune" [30].) In the portrait of Sénécal the narrator seems to ask us to believe in phrenology: "Sénécal—qui avait un crâne en pointe—ne considérait que les systèmes" (58). ("Senecal—who had a pointed skull—valued systems to the exclusion of all else" [68].) In "Le Travail des stéréotypes dans les brouillons de la 'prise des Tuileries' (*L'Education sentimentale*, III, 1),"[5] Anne Herschberg-Pierrot examines the manuscripts of *L'Education* along with the historical accounts used by Flaubert in preparation of the novel and shows how the author self-consciously employs clichés and stereotypes. After analyzing the *brouillons* for the sentence that uses the wave metaphor to describe the people ("flots vertigineux," "un fleuve refoulé par une marée d'équinoxe," *L'Education*, 289–90; 289), she claims that the language of other texts permits the subject who cites "to erase herself behind the citation" (52). She concludes,

> The drafts show an intertextual elaboration of 'sources' that reveals how the stereotypes are points of articulation for a meta-book. The mention of phrases used by historians, the reprise (whether modified or not) of their interpretations of the events, makes *L'Education sentimentale* a "book of books" that can carry them off as well in deriding the citation. (61)[6]

However, the cliché does not just appear in comments on the actions but in the representations. During the description of Mme Arnoux, the narrator invokes a cultural cliché: "D'ailleurs elle touchait au mois d'août des femmes, époque tout à la fois de réflexion et de tendresse, où la maturité qui commence colore le regard d'une femme plus profonde..." (273). ("Besides, she was approaching the August of a woman's life, a period which combines reflection and tenderness, when the maturity which is beginning kindles a warmer flame in the eyes . . ." [272].) This kind of reference to cultural knowledge is one of the props of realistic discourse and one with which Balzacian texts are filled.[7] Comprehension of these generalities is essential to the reader's understanding of the novel. As Barthes says, "Stereotypes are the contemporary path of 'truth,' the way in which the original rhetorical effort is transformed into the canonical, constraining form of the signified."[8] And yet in Flaubert's text the reader must at the same time question the clichés that announce themselves as such, that do not offer the transparence of realistic discourse, and that replace rather than support the representation of experience. A comparison with some passages from *Les Illusions perdues* will illustrate how differently commentary functions in a text that does not question its own language.

When the narrator introduces Lucien de Rubempré, he not only opposes his hero to David Séchard but situates the portrait:

> He was slender but of average height. Any man looking at his feet would have been tempted to take him for a girl in disguise, the more so because, like most men of subtle, not to say astute mind, he had a woman's shapely hips. This is usually reliable as a clue to character [*cet indice, rarement trompeur*] and was so in Lucien's case. (59–60; 27)

The narrator establishes an observer, a narratee, for the reader and then establishes a detail as an index that he asserts is true. The narrator uses examples of common knowledge or generates his own formulas in order to build his fictional world. Moreover, these formulas are reinforced by a variety of persuasive techniques: direct address ("Imaginez cet atelier" [58]; "Imagine the workshop" [25]), assertions ("rarement trompeur"), as well as references to historical places and people. *L'Education* not only questions this kind of discourse but also the other project of the Balzacian text: the creation of a mysterious world "behind" the empirical description of manners.

This brings us to a crucial point in the processes of representation in Balzac, and one which has been developed by Peter Brooks in *The Melodramatic Imagination*. According to Brooks, Balzac postulates two planes of meaning: the world of representation and the world of signification (148). The characters who neglect the plane of representation and attempt direct contact with the world of signification are struck with aphasia and cannot speak (e.g., Louis Lambert, 124).

Balzac's project is "to make the plane of representation imply, suggest, open onto the world of spirit as much as can possibly be managed; to make the vehicles of representation evocative of significant tenors" (125). To establish this point, Brooks opposes the Balzacian novel to the novel of manners. (He cites Marivaux, Laclos, Austen, Stendhal, and Forster.) In the novel of manners, "gestures are counters which have value in terms of a system, a social code which forms their context and assigns their meaning" (131). Although this is useful for distinguishing Balzac's world from that of these novelists, from my point of view on *L'Education sentimentale*, the system of knowledge in which the representation is inscribed (whether social or occult) is less important than the fact that both kinds of novels work within and/or generate these systems. ("Systems of knowledge" means network of referents and significations that define and explain a world.) In the Balzacian *Bildungsroman* Brooks's "level of signification" is mastered by the narrator and by the informed characters (e.g., Vautrin and Mme de Beauséant). In *Le Père Goriot*, a "positive" *Bildungsroman*, Rastignac acquires this knowledge of the world by the end of the novel. As Brooks says, "Rastignac has indeed at the last achieved a position analogous to that of the author: the master of his material, capable of recognizing through the visionary glance, the terms of the true drama hidden behind facades" (140). The connection between vision and mastery is explicitly thematized at the end of the novel when Rastignac looks down on to Paris from Père Lachaise and utters his challenge: " 'A nous deux maintenant.' " In *Les Illusions perdues*, a "negative" *Bildungsroman*, even though Lucien fails to conquer Parisian society and to master fully its meanings, the narrator and the reader have access to this knowledge. In *L'Education*, the narrator does not provide a system of knowledge for the text. The forces of reference explode the realistic system of signification, open a vision that is not contained in the realistic ontology. The narrator does not hold knowledge that the hero seeks to master. The language and ontology of the text are always problematic. In *Les Illusions perdues* the reader's initiation into this system discourages him from questioning individual comments. When Lucien goes to Paris with Mme de Bargeton and no longer sees the same woman he did in Angoulême, the narrator tells us,

> Although Lucien was still bleary-eyed from his sudden awakening, he found Louise scarcely recognizable in this cold, sunless room with its faded curtains, its depressing, overscrubbed

tiles, its worn, tasteless, antequated or secondhand furniture. Indeed certain persons neither look nor are the same once they are detached from the faces, places and objects which constitute their normal environment. . . . This is especially noticeable in the case of provincials. (170; 152)

L'Education sentimentale takes up a similar scene when Frédéric returns to Paris after his inheritance, finds the Arnoux in new lodgings and feels unmoved by the sight of Mme Arnoux: "Frédéric s'était attendu à des spasmes de joie;—mais les passions s'étiolent quand on les dépayse, et ne retrouvant plus Mme Arnoux dans le milieu qu'il l'avait connue, elle lui semblait avoir perdue quelque chose, porter confusément comme une dégradation, enfin n'être plus la même" (109). ("Frédéric had expected to feel paroxysms of joy; but passions wilt when they are transplanted, and finding Madame Arnoux in a setting which was unfamiliar to him, he had the impression that she had somehow lost something, that she had suffered a vague degradation, in short she had changed" [116].) Flaubert's text does not maintain the narrator's englobing perspective. The text moves from exterior focalization in which the narrator is completely effaced to a comment—which is suspended between a dash and an "et" that calls attention to the arbitrariness of the narrative movement—and then glides toward the hero's shapeless impression ("elle lui semblait avoir perdue quelque chose") and his shallow conclusion ("enfin n'être pas la même"). In commenting on the first *Education sentimentale*, Sartre notes that "the passage to the universal is always defensive in Flaubert and is tantamount to a refusal of self-knowledge" (*L'Idiot*, II, 1693). Although Sartre speaks of Flaubert, his remark on the use of the generalization is pertinent to my discussion. The comments of the narrator substitute for the experience of the character. They function for the reader as deictics; that is, the comments do not enrich the representation of experience but replace the representation of experience by saying: "You know, reader, the kind of experience it is." The experience of the character resists formulation. As Sartre says, "comprehension is a silent accompaniment of lived experience, a familiarity of the understanding with itself, a putting into perspective of elements and moments but without explanation. Comprehension is an obscure grasping of the meaning of a process beyond its significations" (II, 1544). This comprehension is opposed to formulated knowledge. According to Sartre, Flaubert believes that "intimate self-knowledge [*connaissance*] is impossible because understanding is not reducible to knowledge of facts [*savoir*]" (II, 1549). In *L'Education*, the narrator's maxims do not enclose the experience of the characters in a fixed ontology and system of knowledge. Maxims do not socialize and universalize the power of subjectivity but gesture weakly at experience that escapes language.

These maxims do not have to be explicit but can be simply referred to by the narrator, as we saw earlier in this chapter. The most grandiose example of such a reference asks the reader to fill in his knowledge of the material that is traditionally the subject of the *Bildungsroman*. At the end of the long scene at Rosanette's salon, a scene in which we see a few of Frédéric's thoughts and many heterogeneous objects (chapter 1 above), we read, "Une autre soif lui était venue, celle des femmes du luxe et de <u>tout ce que comporte l'existence parisienne</u>" (127). ("Another thirst had come upon him: the thirst for women, for luxury, for everything that life in Paris implies" [133].) The topos of knowledge that informs the *Bildungsroman* is reduced to summary that the reader is assumed to know already. What follows is the hero's reverie, not reflections that could enrich the scene. The daydream that floats off independently of the stimulus is Frédéric's most frequently represented mental activity.

These maxims and assumptions on the part of the narrator raise the problem of the text's coherence. Since the commentary does not contain the representation and the narrator supplies no symbolism, the reader looks for a network of causal connections. In *L'Education*, however, the language of causality rarely appears; and if it does, it appears in the character's language, not the narrator's (e.g., "donc," "d'ailleurs," "ainsi," as I noted in the last chapter). The narrator's connections among events are temporal "puis," "alors," "un jour," "souvent," "cependant," and "et," which is a logical and temporal connective, or rather, an unclosed gap in this text. Albert Thibaudet (*Gustave Flaubert*) was the first to remark the unusual use of "et" in Flaubert's novels. Thibaudet notes the "et de mouvement . . . that accompanies or signifies in the course of a description or narration a shift to a sharper emotion, to a more important or dramatic moment, a progression."[9] Thibaudet's suggestive definition covers a variety of uses; however, the common trait among them is the sense of separation rather than conjunction created by the "et," the sense of shift from one autonomous process (event, thing) to another. Thibaudet cites the following example from *L'Education*: "Cependant des nuages s'amoncelaient; le ciel orageux chauffait l'électricité de la multitude, elle tourbillonnaient sur elle-même, indécise, avec un large balancement de houle; et l'on sentait dans ses profondeurs une force, incalculable, et comme l'energie d'un élément." ("In the meantime clouds were piling up; the stormy sky electrified the crowd and it swirled about irresolutely, surging backwards and forwards; in its depths one could sense an incalculable strength, an elemental force.") (Thibaudet, 266; L'Education, 320; 317). The "et" often marks a textual movement that lacks a connection. After a paragraph in the *passé simple*, the reader finds the following one-sentence paragraph: "Et, cherchant ainsi, il élargissait chaque jour sa conception et s'en émerveillait" (150). ("Searching around like this, he expanded his concept every day, marvelling at it as it grew" [154].) After a paragraph of soliloquy, the "et" marks the movement to rationalization in a new one-sentence paragraph: "Et Frédéric s'applaudissait de son indépendance, comme s'il eût refusé un service à M. Dambreuse" (182). ("And Frederic congratulated himself on his independence, as if he had refused Monsieur Dambreuse a favour" [185].)

The narrator's ambiguous status as the source of knowledge and textual unity continues in his use of comparisons. As Proust says, "there is probably not in all of Flaubert a single beautiful metaphor. Moreover, his images are generally so weak that they rarely distinguish themselves from those that his most insignificant characters would come up with" ("A Propos du style de Flaubert," 73). (Proust's examples show that he uses "metaphor" to include analogies.) Although *L'Education* has almost no metaphors, it is full of comparisons; however, these comparisons are primarily clichés that are limited to a phrase or a sentence. Like the comments, these interventions by the narrator, as Proust notes, are as banal as Frédéric's own speech. Their frequency, however, shows that language contains endless similarities, though the banality and frequency of these comparisons lead the reader to question their referential force and their signification. In Proust's and James's metaphors (comparisons) the startling relationships that are produced by the juxtaposition of tenor and vehicle explode the limited signification of the tenor. Moreover, the figures become alternative discourses that are developed for paragraphs or pages, discourses that open new possibilities at the level of reference and signification.[10]

The comparisons in *L'Education* often invoke vague conceptual knowledge rather than visual images, particularly when the comparisons are only lexical: "Ils étaient tristes comme après de grandes débauches" (14) ("They felt sad as if they had been indulging in wild debauchery" [26]); "Il se sentait comme perdu dans un monde lointain" (24) ("He felt as if he were lost in a remote world" [35]). In these examples, the comparisons represent emotions, a domain freed from the language of perception and from the weight of verisimilitude that bears down on description and action, and yet these feelings are named only by allusions to the already known. These references to the familiar are also apparent in the following analogies for events and actions: "Comme un feuillage emporté par un ouragan, son amour disparu" (283) ("And, like a leaf carried away by a hurricane, his love disappeared" [281]); "Comme un architecte qui fait le plan d'un palais, il arrangea, d'avance, sa vie" (101) ("Like an architect, designing a palace, he planned the life he was going to lead" [109]).

The preceding examples also show the presence of clichés or variations on clichés (the flight of love with blown leaves, and the architectural analogy for planning). Amossy and Rosen have some fascinating pages on clichés in the comparisons in *Madame Bovary*.[11] They show how several comparisons in *Madame Bovary* are variations on clichés, where familiar comparisons are changed slightly. For instance, "plus pâle que le satin blanc de sa robe" is derived from "blanche ou pâle comme un linge" (Amossy, 74). The result is that the figure "remains deliberately banal, stuck in the commonplace formulas that gave rise to it, and of which the figure retains the indelible trace" (75). Their conclusion is that "the analogical figures seem to slip back into the ruts of the arrested locution. This incessant referral to the cliché—as if writing could not rid itself of it—determines the status of the comparison and all other figures of analogy."[12]

The narrator thus does not become an ordering authority whose voice unifies the fragments of culture into a text. The text is produced by a shifting polyvalent voice that invokes the known and renders it opaque and fragmented. *L'Education* performs what Roland Barthes calls the task of art: "the task of art is to de-express [*inexprimer*] the expressible" (*Essais critiques*, 14–15).

The absence of a unifying voice raises questions about the text's articulation of meaning. The nature of the text's forces appears against the background of the intertexts that are invoked in the beginning of the novel. The opening of the novel invites the reader to read it as a typical *Bildungsroman*. The subtitle, "l'histoire d'un jeune homme," suggests that the focalization will be on a single character who will be typical ("un jeune homme") and that the plot will unfold chronologically. The opening scene reinforces these expectations by establishing a realistic cadre through physical description, references to historical names (Paris, Quai Saint Bernard) and clear temporal markers ("le 15 septembre 1840 vers six heures du matin"). This scene also engages the expectation of a teleological and dialectical plot. That is, the text will focus on the thoughts, actions, and settings that contribute to the development of the problem of the novel. The problem of *L'Education* is the traditional one of the *Bildungsroman:* the hero's dissatisfaction with his present position and his desire to find an acceptable place in the world. ("Il [Frédéric] trouvait que le bonheur mérité par l'excellence de son âme tardait à venir" [2]; "He considered that the happiness which his nobility of soul deserved was slow in coming" [16].) Following a typical pattern for the genre, the text then moves to a significant moment that projects the hero into action (Frédéric's vision of Mme Arnoux). Once the problem and the trajectory of the plot are established, the text flashes back and fills in the background of the character. In this chapter (I, 2) the protagonist's literary ambitions are reinforced and opposed to those of his friend Deslauriers, who seeks political power. (In *Les Illusions perdues* Lucien is opposed to David Séchard as well as to Parisian foils.) The Balzacian intertext is established not only by the text's form but also by Deslauriers's admonition to Frédéric: " 'Remember Rastignac in *La Comedie humaine*' " (17; 29). Moreover, the object of the hero's quest (Mme Arnoux) and Deslauriers return frequently in the text. This repetition, which is typical of the realistic novel, invites the reader to unify the text by offering occasions for the characters (or narrator) to discuss similarities or continuities in the characters' behavior.[13]

The discourse of the text, however, also lends itself to another reading. Perhaps the most obvious violations of narrative conventions are the use of scene, summary, iteration, and ellipsis. In the novel prior to Flaubert, the iterative representation of events is used to establish a backdrop against which the dramatic action takes place. When compared to the dramatically presented singulative events, the iterative narration does not take up much space in the discourse. That is, in the dramatic presentation the duration of the discourse approaches the duration of the story, whereas in the iterative and summary presentations the duration of the discourse is considerably shorter than the duration of the story. The summary, which is a singulative treatment, is generally used to leap across extensive periods in the story, to serve as a transition between the major scenes. As Gérard Genette says, "Summary remained until the end of the nineteenth century, the most common transition between two scenes, the background against which they detached themselves, and thus the connective link par excellence of the novelistic narrative. The fundamental rhythm of the narrative is the alternation of summary and scene."[14]

Thus, the contrast between the treatment of a series of events in summary or iterative form serves to put these events in the background, to make them less significant than the large scenes. The convention is reinforced by the assumption that the narrator will keep the reader informed about the significant events—in the case of *L'Education*, the hero's motivations for his actions and his reflections on these actions. This assumption permits the reader to conclude that those events or parts of events that are omitted by summary, ellipsis, or paralipsis are not significant. (This information may be delayed for reasons of plot, of course, such as in the mystery novel.)

Flaubert's text upsets these relationships in several ways. First, the use of iterative narration is expanded at the expense of dramatic action. The hero is thus characterized by states of being and by his habits rather than by his unique actions. Since an iterative presentation is synthetic, it suppresses the individuality of actions and foregrounds the codes and the sequence of the actions. Despite this reductive tendency, however, this aspect does permit a wide range of flexibility in the level of abstraction of the information presented as well as in the categories used to characterize a period. Second, the explanatory material that normally links iterative and singulative actions is omitted. Third, the text includes gratuitous incidents that serve no function in the plot. Finally, summary and ellipsis are used to bypass apparently significant periods in the hero's life. In the following example, the narrator uses the imperfect to plunge Frédéric into a circular, undefined temporal period and then moves elliptically to the *passé simple*. The reader must fill in the justification for the action and determine the reasons for the narrator's representation of events:

> Ainsi les jours s'écoulaient, dans la répétition des mêmes ennuis et des habitudes contractées. Il feuilletait des brochures sous les arcades de l'Odéon, allait lire *la Revue des Deux Mondes* au café, entrait dans une salle du Collège de France, écoutait pendant une heure une leçon de chinois ou d'économie politique. Toutes les semaines, il écrivait longuement à Deslauriers, dînait de temps en temps avec Martinon, voyait quelquefois M. de Cisy.
>
> Il loua un piano, et composa des valses allemandes.

> Un soir, au théâtre du Palais-Royal, il aperçut, dans une loge d'avant-scène, Arnoux près d'une femme. (25)

> So the days went by, in the repetition of the same boring activities and the same habits. He glanced through leaflets in the Odeon arcade, read the *Revue des deux mondes* in some café or other, and dropped into the College de France to spend an hour listening to a lecture on Chinese or on political economy. Every week he wrote a long letter to Deslauriers, dined now and then with Martinon, and occasionally saw Monsieur de Cisy.
> He hired a piano and composed German waltzes.
> One evening, at the Théâtre du Palais-Royal, he saw Arnoux in a stage box sitting beside a woman. (37)

After a few short paragraphs relating Frédéric's solution of the mystery, the narrator abruptly summarizes Frédéric's potentially rich experience, giving us enough information to violate the summary convention and to arouse expectations while withholding information about the hero's thoughts:

> L'hiver se termina. Il fut moins triste au printemps, se mit à préparer son examen, et, l'ayant subi d'une façon médiocre, partit ensuite pour Nogent.
> Il n'alla point à Troyes voir son ami, afin d'éviter les observations de sa mère. Puis, à la rentrée, il abandonna son logement et prit, sur le quai Napoléon, deux pièces, qu'il meubla. L'espoir d'une invitation chez les Dambreuse l'avait quitté; sa grande passion pour Mme Arnoux commençait à s'éteindre. (26)

> The winter came to an end. He felt less melancholy in the spring, started working for his examination, passed it without distinction, and then left for Nogent.
> He did not go to Troyes to see his friend, so as to avoid his mother's comments. Then, at the beginning of the next term, he left his lodgings and took a couple of rooms on the Quai Napoleon, which he furnished. He had given up hope of receiving an invitation to the Dambreuse's; and his grand passion for Madame Arnoux was beginning to fade away. (37–38)

During this period, his two purposes for coming to Paris (love and power) have dissolved, and yet we learn only that they have ceased to interest him. The motor of the plot apparently will not depend on the dialectic of the hero's ideas with society; there will be no *Bildung*. Instead, Frédéric's passivity opens up a chain of substitution of signs that is not closed into thematic unity or knowledge.

This centrifugal movement of the text is reinforced by the frequent appearance of chance.[15] The unfolding of the plot does not follow a teleology of the hero's life or of social forces named by the narrator. That is, Frédéric's interrupted and abandoned projects provide no purposive link among events, and the narrator's representation of the surrounding forces does not supplement the hero's inconsistency by attributing intentionality to society. Chance thus takes on a force that is not present in Balzac, as the following remark by Georg Lukács on *Les Illusions perdues* makes clear: "Breadth is . . . required to exclude the element of chance from that accidental intertwinement of persons and events which Balzac, like every other great epic poet, uses with such sovereign superiority. Only a great wealth of multiple connections affords sufficient elbow-room in which chance can become artistically productive and ultimately lose its fortuitous character" (*Studies*, 55). Chance is integrated into the forces of unity not by simple causality but by a large web of relations: "the necessity which nullifies chance consists of an intricate network of causal connections and . . . the aggregate necessity of an entire trend of developments constitutes poetic necessity" (*Studies*, 56). *Les Illusions perdues* presents a network that recuperates chance: "Balzac creates a wide space within which hundreds of accidents may intersect each other and yet in their aggregate produce fateful necessities" (56–57). The narrator and the characters explain in the same ways as does Lukács: "Lucien was waiting for some stroke of luck (un hasard) which did not come off. In Paris, such luck (hasard) only comes to people who move around a great deal: the number of relationships increases the chances of success in every sphere, and moreover luck (hasard) is on the side of the big battalions" (211; 198). When Lousteau explains the nature of literary success to Lucien, chance is given a large role, but it does not escape the system: "The attainment of this brilliant zenith depends on so many and so rapidly varying chances (accidents) that no example has occurred of two men reaching it by the same route" (253; 248).

The presence of these decentering forces raises the question of irony, one of the principal elements of the New Critical reading of *L'Education*. According to this reading, the narrator and/or Flaubert savagely exposes the stupidities (political, literary, social clichés) of

The Refusal of Authority 49

the generation of 1848 or of humanity in general. The foundations for such a reading are the authority of the narrator or author (the power of his language to master the world of the novel, to unmask the characters) and the reader's conception of "real" people. That is, the reader assumes that the text is a realistic one, that it is appropriate to compare his model of humanity with the one presented in the text. Thus, he is able to assert his superiority (and that of others) to Frédéric. This view also permits the reader to identify with the narrator. The invocation of such a model of humanity is implicit in the ironic mode, as Northrop Frye points out: "If inferior in power or intelligence to ourselves, so that we have the sense of looking down on a scene of bondage, frustration, or absurdity, the hero belongs to the *ironic mode.*"[16] Before considering the appropriateness of these two criteria, I shall look at a series of Frédéric's actions that are "obviously" ironic according to this reading.

The sequence begins when Frédéric is rescued from a period of *ennui* by a letter from Deslauriers ("Alors, il se rejeta violemment sur cette affection plus solide, et plus haute" [43]; "In a violent reaction he fell back on this stronger and loftier band of affection" [54]). Before Deslauriers's arrival (next paragraph), Frédéric gets an invitation to dinner from Jacques Arnoux, and he abandons his higher affection. At this dinner he gets a handshake from the hostess, and this touches off the ecstasy for which he has been waiting: "He was no longer aware of his surroundings, of space, of anything. . . . Then he was seized by one of those tremors of the soul in which one seems to be transported into a higher world" [*un des frissons de l'âme où il vous semble qu'on est transporté dans un monde supérieur*] (50; 60–61). He interprets this experience of value as a testimony to his capabilities and to his unsullied future:

> Une faculté extraordinaire, dont il ne savait pas l'objet, lui était venue. Il se demanda, sérieusement, s'il serait un grand peintre ou un grand poète;—et il se décida pour la peinture, car les exigences de ce métier le rapprocheraient de Mme Arnoux. Il avait donc trouvé sa vocation! Le but de son existence était clair maintenant, et l'avenir infaillible. (50)

> He had been endowed with an extraordinary talent, the object of which he did not know. He asked himself in all seriousness whether he was to be a great painter or a great poet; and he decided in favour of painting, for the demands of this profession would bring him closer to Madame Arnoux. So he had

found his vocation! The object of his existence was now clear, and there could be no doubt about the future. (61)

Rarely does the narrator seem to insist on our ironic response with such forcefulness as in this last passage. The grandiose terms "un grand peintre ou un grand poète" contrast with our conception of the protagonist (intratextual perspective of the character), and the rapidity and certainty of the decision contrast with our sense of a normal deliberation time for this kind of decision (the text's relationship to cultural models). Further, the narrator invites this kind of ironic reading with his "sérieusement" and by his refusal to indicate how much time passes during Frédéric's reflections or what his thoughts are. Both are represented by a dash. As opposed to Lucien's extended inner debates, Frédéric's interior life appears only in brief phrases or not at all.

But this reading can be reversed. The reader is invited to share common experience with Frédéric and the narrator: "où il vous semble qu'on est transporté dans un monde supérieur." The narrator does not offer a transcendent position with which the reader can identify. The reader can, of course, always assert his superiority to Frédéric—i.e., invoke the criterion of Frye's ironic mode; however, such an assertion would be much like maintaining one's superiority to Beckett's Vladimir and Estragon or Kafka's Gregor Samsa. Frédéric's stupidities are like the lapses in memory of Beckett's characters. Certainly, Frédéric appears as an object of irony if one reads with Balzacian realistic intertexts; but if these models of texts and humanity are suspended, the irony is replaced by a Beckettian comedy. The reader cannot escape from the world of the novel by attributing the hero's weaknesses to the accidental features of his personality or his culture. In a novelistic world where the environment appears as hallucinatory objects that resist the comprehension of the characters and the reader, where speech and consciousness are infected by opaque formulas, the reader would have to be nonhuman not to be implicated. The text represents particulars that refuse to remain within the known, that claim universality and that resist assimilation into a universal system.[17] Once we remove Frédéric from the Balzacian context that invites us to smile at the poverty of his mind and personality, the representation of his experience takes on a new interest. This is the subject of the next chapter.

4
Character: Frédéric Moreau and the *Bildungsroman*

I

CRITICS have approached the hero of the novel from two points of view. One is a realistic reading that treats him as an effete, ineffectual bourgeois who is infused with Romantic platitudes. That is, he is read in the same way as is a Balzacian hero. The other approach, proposed by Robbe-Grillet and Culler, is that Frédéric is a cipher, an anticharacter who anticipates the characters in the *nouveau roman*, a reading that reduces the power of the text to antinovelistic dimensions. I propose another way of looking at Frédéric, a way that looks at him as the site for the play of language and silence that anticipates Beckett, not Robbe-Grillet. In *Novembre*, the character is his own narrator (until the last section), and he confronts the difficulty of articulating his own experience under the weight of the cliché. This, as Shoshana Felman suggests (*La Folie et la chose littéraire*, 192), is Flaubert's *L'Innommable*. Frédéric, however, is a completely naive hero who never reflects on the poverty of his language or the problematic nature of his being. He is caught in a Beckettian world, but he cannot articulate his predicament. He is Flaubert's Winnie in *Happy Days*, and like Winnie and her black sack full of objects, Frédéric is confronted with hard, recalcitrant signifiers that he must convert into signs: sensations from the exterior world (both people and things), spoken words, and memories.

Frédéric's response to these three types of signals can be divided into three groups: action, ecstasy (usually followed by a reverie), in which the exterior world and his personality disappear, or nothing (i.e., the signifier remains just that for the character). None of these responses builds on the past. Each moment is on the same "level" and exists only in the present. Therefore, Frédéric's passivity cannot be written off as simply a particular psychological trait of a realistic character; passivity is part of reconsideration of the relationship between desire and signs that is present in all of Flaubert. In Balzac, passion and human nature exist independently of signs—even if language influences them—and the language of the text reveals these characteristics to the reader. In *Madame Bovary* signs generate passion (e.g., her reading) as much as they shape it. In *L'Education sentimentale*, signs are not so successful in generating or containing desire, and they are not mastered by the will and consciousness of the character. To show the originality of *L'Education*, I shall examine the text's treatment of the *Bildungsroman*'s development around conflicting interests; and then I shall look at the representation of moments outside the language of means and ends.

The presentation of conflict in the realistic *Bildungsroman* reveals the argumentative and conceptual concerns of the text—that is, its concentration on problems of concepts and knowledge within a fixed ontology. In *Les Illusions perdues*, significant events are marked not only by the narrator's comments—e.g., "one of those events which entirely change the look of things in a small town" (144; 125)—but by the representation of the hero's dialogue with himself and others. The scene that follows (Lucien's appearance at Mme de Bargeton's salon) takes up twenty pages. Even in less definitive moments, such as Lucien's rationalization of Coralie's relationship with Camusot, we see the hero articulate his reasons. When the hero's choice is decisive, the text establishes the forces on each side. For example, when Lucien must choose between following his art by staying with the ethically pure and brilliant Cénacle or by following his economic and social ambitions through journalism, we read: "He did not know he had to choose between two different paths, two systems for which the Cénacle and journalism respectively stood" (257; 252). Although the character's speech and action are always supplemented in Balzac's text by the narrator's commentary, Lucien remains a psychological presence through the dramatic representation of his speech and thought and through his decision-making. Society is dramatized not only by the opposition between the worlds of d'Arthez and Lousteau but also in the power of society to change the lovers. When Lucien and Mme de Bargeton come to Paris, the narrator prepares the reader for the changes in their ideas: "In the case of both Madame de Bargeton and Lucien, mutual disenchantment was setting in, and Paris was the cause of it" (179; 162). Lukács describes this interaction of the particular and the general in *Les Illusions perdues:*

> The characters and situations are always determined by the totality of the socially decisive forces, but never simply and never directly. For this reason this so completely universal novel is at the same time the story of one particular individual, an individual different from all others. Lucien de Rubempré, on the stage, seems to react independently to the internal and external forces which hamper his rise and which help or hinder him as a result of apparently fortuitous personal circumstances or passions, but which, whatever form they take, always spring from the same social environment which determines his aspirations and ambition. (*Studies*, 53–54)

In *L'Education*, Frédéric's principal competing interests are his love for Mme Arnoux and his desire for social success, which is closely associated with his friendship with Deslauriers. However, his movements between these poles, movements that, according to the conventions of the genre, should be placed in an argumentative/causal scheme, are not developed.

In the opening scene, Frédéric meets Mme Arnoux and decides to pursue her with all the ardor of a Romantic hero. However, when he goes to Paris only two months later, he forgets to go see her until he stumbles on Arnoux's shop: "Comment n'avait-il pas songé à elle, plus tôt, la faute venait de Deslauriers et il s'avança vers la boutique..." (21). ("Why had he not thought of her earlier? It was Deslauriers' fault. He went over to the shop..." [32].) The causal ellipsis between the two parts of the sentence is marked only by "et," where the focalization shifts from interior to exterior. Frédéric does not reflect on his problems; rather, his mind is the site for the appearance of a signifier that opens up possible courses of action or a channel to his interior world. When he finds that Mme Arnoux is not at home, he takes up the social and cultural activities that are traditionally treated as discoveries for the young provincial. This opposition between the expectation of the hero and the existing society begins the dialectic of "knowledge" that is developed both by the narrator and by the character's own language. In *L'Education,* however, this topos is suspended. The dialectic is merely a substitution; no third synthetic term arises; nothing is learned and yet the hero is not ill at ease or at a disadvantage with respect to the other characters. The plot advances only when Frédéric feels himself in contact with himself or the world. Therefore, if he undertakes potentially interesting subjects, and they do not touch off one of these feelings, his activities are presented in the summary: "Les joies qu'il s'était promises n'arrivaient pas; et, quand il eut épuisé un cabinet de lecture, parcouru les collections du Louvre et plusieurs fois de suite été au spectacle, il tomba dans un désoeuvrement sans fond" (22). ("The joys he had looked forward to failed to materialize; and after exhausting the resources of a lending-library, inspecting the collections at the Louvre, and going to the theatre several nights in succession, he lapsed into a state of lethargy" [33].) In *L'Education* society is indexed for the reader by the narrator's portraits and descriptions and the reported dialogues. However, society does not make itself known; it is *already* known. The codes that appear are just linguistic matter that the reader must convert into knowledge, knowledge that the text devalues and subverts.

In the next chapter, we see Frédéric visit the Arnoux regularly until he becomes disgusted with the milieu. Chance, in the form of a letter from Deslauriers, gives him the opportunity to try another course of action: "In a violent reaction he fell back on this stronger and loftier band of affection. A man like Deslauriers was worth all the women in the world. From now on he would have no further need of Regimbard, Pellerin, Hussonet, or anybody else" (43; 54). A similar sequence in II, 1, when Frédéric returns to Paris after his inheritance, is full of dreams of his future life with Mme Arnoux. However, when he sees Mme Arnoux and is unmoved, the reader finds only a superficial remark by the narrator, as we saw in chapter 3, and a shift of the focalization to Frédéric: "Frédéric s'était attendu à des spasmes de joie;—mais les passions s'étiolent quand on les dépayse, et ne retrouvant plus Mme Arnoux dans le milieu qu'il l'avait connue, elle lui semblait avoir perdu quelque chose, porter confusément comme une dégradation, enfin n'être plus la même" (109). ("Frederic had expected to feel paroxysms of joy; but passions wilt when they are transplanted, and finding Madame Arnoux in a setting which was unfamiliar to him, he had the impression that she had somehow lost something, that she had suffered a vague degradation, in short that she had changed" [116].) The causal ellipsis marked by an "et," blank space, or a merely temporal marker followed by a brief, shallow passage of psychological narration, FID, or an action often marks shifts in the hero's interest. At other times, he forgets Mme Arnoux until he happens to see her. (Business takes him to Arnoux's shop [268; 266]; he meets her at a party [342; 339].)

FID frequently appears with the narrator's elliptical summary in these apparently crucial moments. However, these passages do not explore the psychological complexity of the hero; instead, they mark the presence of a short sequence of reasoning or a cliché, a public rather than private expression. This reasoning propels the hero into the next course of action. For example, Frédéric's choice of profession is represented in summarized narration followed by FID in a passage cited in the previous chapter: "et il se décida pour la peinture, car les exigences de ce métier le rapprocheraient de Mme Arnoux. Il avait donc trouvé sa vocation! Le but de son existence était clair maintenant, et l'avenir infaillible" (50). ("and he decided in favour of painting, for the demands of this profession would bring him closer to Madame Arnoux. So he had found his vocation! The object of his existence was now clear, and there could be no doubt about the future" [61]). He abandons painting in the next chapter without a remark. When he decides to give up his siege of Mme Arnoux after she misses their rendez-vous, we read, "This was pushing insolence too far! He was filled with angry pride. He swore to himself that he would never again feel the slightest desire of her" (283; 281). When his political aspirations are crushed at the Club de l'Intelligence, we find only, "Puis il éprouva le besoin de voir Rosanette. Après tant de laideurs et d'emphase, sa gentille personne serait un délassement" (310). ("Then he felt an urge to see Rosanette. After all the ugliness and bombast, her prettiness would be a relief" [307].) The representation of Frédéric's consciousness provides no argumentative language that assembles society or his pursuits; and, as we saw in the previous chapter, the narrator offers no such language. Moreover, the burden of these passages of FID is "increased"—in comparison with *Les Illusions perdues*—by the sheer quantity of Frédéric's changes of direction.

The text thus refuses to give the narrator or the character the power to argue from a fixed ontology of the self or the world. There is no determining instinct or passion beneath the character's roles, nor is the hero assimilated into social forces such as those Lukács describes in Balzac. "Frédéric" becomes the locus where the cultural codes are played out, where language is not an instrument of the subject but a force that hurls the hero through space and time. The powers of this universe are the cliché and the accident. The cliché appears at significant moments and stimulates in the hero a novelistic teleology for his life. These clichés never sustain the hero for very long. They quickly dissipate or they are abandoned and replaced by another future. Unlike traditional heroes, Flaubert's protagonist is not impelled by social or psychological causes. He recovers from nothingness by wandering the streets or casting about among his friends until he is invaded by another of society's value-clichés that he can apply to his situation. Thus, accident takes the place of purposeful action in the plot; Frédéric (human nature) is divested of its causative force. But this does not mean that Frédéric is caught in a determinative social, biological, or metaphysical force as in Balzac and Zola, for Flaubert's text destabilizes not only the hero but the society. There is no opposition between self and other, for otherness has invaded the self. However, the novel not only breaks the ontology of realism by undermining the language of means and ends; the text also represents moments that escape its strictures and open on an uncharted world.

II

Even though the plot resists the argumentative language of "turning points," there are nonetheless "privileged" moments in the text, moments that escape the language of concepts. These moments are not marked by large scenes, commentary, or reflections but by silence and reverie. During these moments the hero experiences a liberation from the struggle of subject and object and another world is opened.

Some of these reveries are stimulated by an external object; however, they do not engage the object but float off independently of the stimulus, and they usually work within *lieux communs*, standard romantic topoi. For example, at Rosanette's party, Frédéric observes a series of women: "the women passed him in a single dazzling vision, each with her distinctive beauty exciting a different emotion" (120; 126). What follows is not a taxonomy of beauty but a sequence of imaginary scenes solicited by perception:

> The Polish girl, surrendering languidly to the music, made him long to hold her to his heart while the two of them travelled in a sleigh across a snow-covered plain. The Swiss girl, waltzing with her body erect and her eyelids lowered, opened up vistas of tranquil pleasure in a lakeside chalet. Then, all of a sudden, the Bacchante, leaning her dark head backwards, made him dream of greedy kisses in oleander

groves, in stormy weather, to the dull beat of tambors. (120; 126–27)

The associative power of an object can stimulate an exotic reverie that has little connection to Frédéric's situation:

> When he went to the Jardin des Plantes, the sight of a palm-tree carried him off to distant lands. They travelled together on the backs of dromedaries, under the awnings of elephants, in the calm of a yacht among blue archipelagoes, or side by side on a couple of mules with bells on their harness, which stumbled over broken pillars in the grass.[1] (68–69; 78)

If these reveries seem to be gratuitous production of images, of significations without referential weight, Frédéric's experiences with Madame Arnoux do not fall so easily into this category. In the opening scene of the novel, Mme Arnoux's appearance wrests Frédéric from his reflections and we read in an isolated paragraph, "Ce fut comme une apparition" (4). ("It was like a vision" [18].) The "ce" has no antecedent, and we learn in the next paragraph some of the impressions that subsequently appear in the hero's consciousness. The "ce" is not named and not nameable, and the narrator intervenes with a comparison. The blank space that separates this sentence from what follows emphasizes both the duration and the inexpressibility of the experience. It is like Kant's description of the sublime in which the imagination is overpowered by a vision.[2] In the next paragraph, Frédéric's contemplation of Mme Arnoux is represented in the language of perception, but this contemplation solicits the desire for knowledge of all that surrounds her, a metonymic displacement of the original experience: "and even the desire for physical possession gave way to a profounder yearning, a poignant curiosity which knew no bounds" (5; 18). Frédéric articulates his experience only after Madame Arnoux has left, and this formulation into clichés produces another ecstatic experience and a reverie. The text first lends itself to Frédéric's subjectivity and then shifts outside of him. The movement is marked here and elsewhere by "et":

> Elle ressemblait aux femmes des livres romantiques. Il n'aurait voulu rien ajouter, rien retrancher à sa personne. L'univers venait tout à coup de s'élargir. Elle était le point lumineux où l'ensemble des choses convergeait;—et bercé par

le mouvement de la voiture, les paupières à demi closes, le regard dans les nuages, il s'abandonnait à une joie rêveuse et infinie.³ (9)

She looked like the women in romantic novels. He would not have wanted to add anything to her appearance, or to take anything away. His world had suddenly grown bigger. She was the point of light on which all things converged; and lulled by the movement of the carriage, his eyelids half closed, his gaze directed at the clouds, he gave himself up to an infinite, dreamy joy. (22)

Language itself can generate an ecstatic experience that opens the possibility for a reverie. Here visual and verbal signs coalesce in the discovery. Note that the reader does not see Frédéric's imagination in action, that there is no tension between the remembered images and the literary models evoked in the present. As we will see, this is typical of the functioning of memory in the novel. That is, memory does not "recover" or preserve the past but serves only as a stimulus in the present. Bachelard notes, "As soon as the world is opened by an image, the dreamer of the world lives the world that has just been offered to him" (150). In this creation, "His cogito is not divided into the dialectic of subject and object" (136).

A similar sequence occurs in I, 3, when Frédéric dines *chez* Arnoux and he shakes Madame's hand: "and he felt as if it were something permeating every particle of his skin" (49; 60). In the next paragraph (next sentence), he walks through the streets of Paris. We read a description of what he sees, and these perceptions stimulate a thought that raises him to ecstasy. The arbitrariness of the link between perception and thought is marked by an "et":

Les rues étaient désertes. Quelquefois une charette lourde passait, en ébranlant les pavés. Les maisons se succédaient avec leurs façades grises, leurs fenêtres closes; et il songeait dédaigneusement à tous ces êtres humains couchés derrière ces murs, qui existaient sans la voir, et dont pas un même ne se doutait qu'elle vécût! Il n'avait plus de conscience du milieu, de l'espace, de rien. (50)

The streets were deserted. Now and then a heavy cart rolled by, shaking the roadway. He passed rows of houses with grey fronts and closed shutters; and he thought disdainfully of all the human beings lying asleep behind those walls, who lived without seeing her, and not one of whom even knew that she existed. He was no longer aware of his surroundings, of space, of anything. (60)

After he walks a bit farther a church bell sounds and he is transported again: "Alors, il fut saisi par un de ces frissons de l'âme où il vous semble qu'on est transporté dans un monde supérieur" (50). ("Then he was seized by one of those tremors of the soul in which one seems to be transported into a higher world" [61].) The pattern is the same: Frédéric undergoes an experience that is outside language and that the narrator represents by a comparison or by an appeal to the reader's experience. The ecstatic feelings that arrive without the mediation of language are then reproduced and displaced either by verbal or sensory signs. "Madame Arnoux" is thus an unstable sign at the level of reference and signification. At some moments the world unleashes an associative burst of signification that also opens referential possibilities (i.e., her physical and moral presence). At others, a referential vision explodes signification. What she is for him changes, and the force of these changes is ontological. "Looking at this woman had an enervating effect on him, like a scent that is too strong. The sensation penetrated to the very depths of his being, and became almost a habitual condition, a new mode of existence" (68; 78).

The discontinuous nature of being, the chain of substitutions, which is the motor of the plot, can be seen by following Frédéric's interest in her. The only time that Mme Arnoux is a unique presence is in the first sentence that refers to her ("Ce fut comme une apparition"). Frédéric immediately likens her to women in other novels ("Elle ressemblait aux femmes des livres romantiques"). When he contemplates her subsequently, she is never free from "otherness," from comparison with other people and things. Even before Frédéric meets Rosanette, he sees her in other women and objects: "each and every woman reminded him of her, through some resemblance or some violent contrast . . .; every street led towards her house. . . . Paris depended on her person, and the great city, with all its voices, thundered like an immense orchestra about her" (68; 78). He also projects her into painting and narratives: "he substituted her for the figures in the paintings" (69; 78). When she visits Frédéric in his apartment (II, 3), Frédéric feels ecstasy only when she has left and he can contemplate her through the furniture that she has touched:

> Back in his study, he gazed at the armchair in which she had sat, and at all the things she had touched. Something of

her hovered in the air around him. The soft caress of her presence lingered on.

"So she has been here!" he said to himself.

And waves of infinite tenderness engulfed him. (188; 190–91)

Like other critics, Jean-Pierre Richard finds Mme Arnoux at the center of the disorder in Frédéric's life: "Although all the moments of his life seem dispersed, each event in its place and moment illustrates the pre-eminence of the unique first moment when Frédéric met Madame Arnoux. All the succeeding episodes of his life will be lived out in relation to this moment."[4]

However, this reading resembles Frédéric's reading of his own life. Richard and Frédéric see Mme Arnoux as the privileged part of these comparisons, as the englobing significance. But these comparisons *are* Mme Arnoux. The proper name "Mme Arnoux" has little signification independently of the comparisons that invade it. Even the referential force of the name changes. Certainly, the name locates the same physical body for Frédéric and for other characters. However, the name does not locate the same being. For others, Mme Arnoux is a completely ordinary woman; for Frédéric, she is an unstable, discontinuous being who does not maintain her autonomy. He even agrees with the judgment of others at certain moments ("quelle bourgeoise" [109]; "what an ordinary creature she is" [117]). What awakens and briefly sustains Frédéric's desire is her otherness.[5]

The possibilities for substitution are increased as Frédéric is drawn into other milieux. After Jacques Arnoux starts taking the hero with him to see Rosanette, Frédéric begins to confound his first love with his new interest: "The company of these two women made as it were two melodies in his life: the one playful, wild, amusing; the other grave and almost religious. And the two melodies, sounding at the same time, swelled continually and gradually intermingled . . ." (145; 149). "This confusion was brought about by similarities between the two establishments" (145; 150). Thus, Mme Arnoux's uniqueness dissolves in comparisons. Signification is threatened not only by irresolvable heterogeneity but also by proliferating similarities, similarities that dissolve the oppositions on which signification is based. Frédéric's loves are usually not concurrent but successive. The hero is rescued from the dissolution of one affair by the appearance of another possibility. (Frustrated by Mme Arnoux, Frédéric goes to Rosanette [210; 212]; at the end of Part II, he sleeps with Rosanette in the room that he had rented for Mme Arnoux; after his failure at the Club de l'Intelligence, he goes to see Rosanette. Then his boredom with Rosanette leads to his affair with Mme Dambreuse.) During these various affairs, Frédéric remembers or is reminded of other loves, particularly his love for Mme Arnoux: "He made use of his old love. He told her about all the emotions which Madame Arnoux had once aroused in him . . ." (365–66; 361). When someone mentions the name "Roque," Frédéric evokes Louise and nights spent with her. Then these nights lead him to think of Mme Arnoux (162; 165).

Memory does not provoke a synthesis, a language that embraces past and present. Memory serves only to touch off a new horizontal movement—that is, either an action or a thought. The past is never understood in the present; there is only the evocation of similarity among sensations, similarities that set off endless metonymic chains and that dissolve all distinctions: "But gradually his hopes and memories, Nogent, the Rue de Choiseul, Madame Arnoux, his mother, all merged together in his mind" (102; 109).

These silences in Flaubert, however, are not like the silences in Balzac. In Balzac silence is focused on a gesture whose significance is outside the power of language, though not outside the knowledge accessible to the narrator. Peter Brooks, who treats gesture in Balzac extensively, says that it is a "device toward the representation of conditions, concepts and forces held to be beyond the possibilities of rational apprehension and literal statement" (77). Usually, however, these gestures are "read" or allegorized even if they are not described. For example, Rastignac sees Mme de Beauséant make a "short gesture" that reveals "the iron fist under the glove." In *Facino Cane*, we read: "He made a frightening gesture of extinguished patriotism and disgust for things human" (cited in Brooks, 76).

In *L'Education*, silence is not provoked by the "meaning" of an action, nor is it focused on the gesture of a character or assimilated into allegorical codes. Silence is the experience of ecstasy touched by differences, an experience that is not translatable into a gesture or into a propositional or mythical statement.

There are not only silences of plenitude but silences of absence and despair. These silences are often marked by the *passé simple*, the indication of the limitlessness of the emotion, and the end of the paragraph—that is, a semantic and temporal ellipsis. Frédéric starts to write a novel but is discouraged when he sees how conventional it is: "The echoes from other writers which he noticed in his novel discouraged him; he dropped it, and his feeling of aimlessness grew worse" (25; 36).

Frédéric does not ruminate on his despair; rather, we see the emptiness hover over a series of repeated actions that "exemplify" the emptiness. In the above example, Frédéric's "désoeuvrement" is limited to a paragraph. However, in other periods the narrator summarizes a period in the *passé simple* and then devotes several pages to the repeated actions that characterize this period:

> Alors commencèrent trois mois d'ennui. Comme il n'avait aucun travail, son désoeuvrement renforçait sa tristesse.
> Il passait des heures à regarder, du haut de son balcon. . . .
> Il rentrait dans sa chambre. . . .
> Il remontait, au hasard, le quartier latin. (64–65)

> Then began three months of boredom. As he had nothing to do, his idleness intensified his melancholy.
> He spent hours on his balcony looking down. . . .
> He would go back to his room. . . .
> He sauntered idly up the Latin Quarter. (74–75)

At the beginning of II, 3, we read:

> Alors commença pour Frédéric une existence misérable. Il fut le parasite de la maison.
> Si quelqu'un était indisposé, il venait trois fois par jour. (170)

> A wretched existence now began for Frédéric. He was the parasite of the house.
> If anybody in the family was ill, he would call three times a day. (173)

The circular time of the iteration weighed down by desperation charges the shift to the singulative with a special force. The character tries to escape from the treadmill, to project a future. Thus, the following passage (cited in the preceding chapter) can now be read not just as a violation of narrative conventions or as an ironic treatment of the hero but as a movement of language and silence:

> Ainsi les jours s'écoulaient dans la répétition des mêmes ennuis et des habitudes contractées. Il feuilletait des bro-

chures sous les arcades de l'Odéon, allait lire *la Revue des Deux Mondes* au café . . . voyait quelquefois M. de Cisy.
Il loua un piano, et composa des valses allemandes.
Un soir. . . (25)

So the days went by, in the repetition of the same boring activities and same habits. He glanced through leaflets in the Odéon arcade, read the *Revue des Deux Mondes* in some café . . . occasionally saw Monsieur de Cisy.
He hired a piano and composed some German waltzes.
One evening. . . (36)

The external focalization, the isolation of the sentence, and the ellipsis and paralipsis mark the failure of this attempt to get out of dizzying repetition.

The most famous use of ellipsis and paralipsis of this kind is at the beginning of III, 6, a passage that Proust was the first to point out (in "A propos du style de Flaubert"): "But in Balzac these temporal shifts have an active and documentary character. Flaubert is the first to free them from the parasitism of the anecdote and the slag of history. He is the first to make these shifts musical" (85). Balzac's summaries follow the conventions of historical and realistic narratives, where the function of summary is simply to leap across time and not to give time an expressive value. For Proust, these temporal movements are the most beautiful thing in the novel: "To my mind, the most beautiful thing about *L'Education sentimentale* is not a sentence but a blank space" (84). In the last line of III, 5, Frédéric sees Sénécal kill Dussardier at the time of the counterrevolution in 1851. III, 6 opens:

>Il voyagea.
>Il connut la mélancholie des paquebots, les froids réveils sous la tente, l'étourdissement des paysages et des ruines, l'amertume des sympathies interrompues.
>Il revint.
>Il fréquenta le monde. (419)

>He travelled.
>He came to know the melancholy of the steamboat, the cold awakening in the tent, the tedium of landscapes and ruins, the bitterness of interrupted friendships.
>He returned.
>He went into society. (411)

The first sentence opens and closes in an indeterminate time but within a familiar semantic space. Frédéric is hurtled out of the Revolution into the "vide." The next sentence represents the period in terms of knowledge of romantic clichés that assert their uniqueness through the definite article and that assume the reader's comprehension. (The definite article functions like a demonstrative adjective, like a deictic.)

L'Education's singular style wrenches the reader from his familiar realistic intertexts. This style is not just a formal beauty—indeed, many readers, including James, find the "continuous, monotonous, lugubrious procession" ("A propos," [74]) incomprehensible—but a unique vision. That is, it is not a point of view on reality but a reconstitution of the nature of reality. Proust applies the word "vision" to Flaubert's novels in precisely this ontological sense: "someone whose completely new and personal use of the indefinite past, the present participle, of certain pronouns and certain prepositions has renewed our vision of things as much as Kant's Categories, his theories of Knowledge and of exterior Reality" ("A propos," 72).

III

The last two scenes of the novel, in which the three main characters meet again after sixteen years and cast retrospective glances over the courses of their lives, open the specular possibilities of the text. In the first of these scenes Mme Arnoux comes to visit Frédéric "vers la fin de mars 1867." The two former lovers tell each other the story of the past and thus become narrators of their own lives ("Ils se racontèrent leurs anciens jours" [421]; "they talked about old times together" [413]). They both self-consciously employ literary analogies: " 'When I read about love in a book, I feel that you are there beside me' " (421; 413). Frédéric replies that he is now able to understand the so-called exaggerated literary representation of passion and thus reverses his earlier pattern. Instead of seeking to find the equivalents of literature in life, he discovers that life makes literature comprehensible: " 'You have made me feel all the things in books which people criticize as exaggerated.' " The intervention of the otherness of language in this intimate moment appears not only through literary allusions but in their address to each other. Madame Arnoux cries out when they first meet and hold hands, "—C'est lui, c'est donc lui" (419). (" 'It's he! Yes, it's he!' ") Later in the scene she says, "—à mon âge, lui! Frédéric" (422). (" 'At my age! Him! Frédéric!' " [414]). The language nonetheless gives them the

Frédéric Moreau and the Bildungsroman   65

feeling that their past is redeemed: "Il ne regretta rien. Ses souffrances d'autrefois étaient payées" (422). ("He regretted nothing. His former sufferings were redeemed" [414].) The feeling of redemption depends on the effacement of the present, of the narrative instance. This effort appears both in the use of third-person pronouns and in Mme Arnoux's use of the future perfect in order to get a retrospective view on the present: " 'Nous nous serons bien aimés!' "[6] (Baldick translates this "we have loved each other well" instead of "we will have loved each other well.") (One might expect the past conditional here, where she asserts that they would have loved each other if it were not for some contingent circumstance.)

Frédéric is forced to confront the narrative instance of their stories when Mme Arnoux takes off her hat and reveals her white hair. For the hero, "It was like a blow in the chest" (421; 414). There is no past in the text. Each moment creates an unbridgeable gulf from its predecessor. Retrospection does not create an englobing perspective from which to tell (write) a story. The creation and collapse of the characters' stories touch the central problem of the text: the difficulty of writing this text when time destroys continuity, when language offers only stale fragments of meaning and when subjectivity flickers in the space of desire. Frédéric is not the tortured protagonist of *L'Innommable*, however. He falls to his knees and chants romantic clichés about how beautiful she *was* (" 'Vous me faisiez l'effet d'un clair de lune par une nuit d'été, quand tout est parfums ... ' " [422]; " 'The effect you had on me was that of a moonlit night in summer ... ' " [414]), and the pressure of the present reality momentarily disappears: "She accepted this adoration of the woman she had ceased to be. Frédéric, drunk with his own eloquences, began to believe what he was saying" (422; 414). The repetition of formulas is a prayer for the liberation from *le mal* that inhabits the world.

The use of *mise en abyme* emerges again in the last scene of the novel, where Frédéric and Deslauriers meet and review their lives. The scene provides a perfect opportunity to use the long temporal sweep of the *Bildungsroman* to compare the different paths taken by the hero and his friend and to develop the interaction of their different ideological positions with each other and with society. The narrator begins by tempting the reader with a tautological explanation, for he says that the two friends are "réconciliés encore une fois, par la fatalité de leur nature qui les faisait toujours se rejoindre et s'aimer" (424). ("reconciled once again by that irresistible element in their nature which always reunited them in friendship" [416].) They are reconciled because they are reconciled.

This reconciliation is a repetition of their reconciliations throughout the novel. The two of them have been in almost constant disagreement about love, politics, and friends, and they have betrayed each other several times. Even when they are intimate, their intimacy results from a frustration by society. Then, they use each other as an audience for their very different dreams. These differences are never overcome through discussion, understanding or personal transcendence; they are just forgotten. The trivialization of differences is part of the ontology of evil that infects language and the world. Heterogeneity cannot be surmounted by analysis but is part of being. In this scene, the two friends survey their pasts for the first time. After several anecdotes, they turn to an examination of the full scope of their lives and the reason for their failure:

> Et ils résumèrent leur vie.
> Ils l'avaient manquée tous les deux, celui qui avait rêvé l'amour, celui qui avait rêvé le pouvoir. Quelle en était la raison?
> ——C'est peut-être le défaut de ligne droite, dit Frédéric.
> ——Pour toi, cela se peut. Moi, au contraire, j'ai péché par excès de rectitude, sans tenir compte de mille choses secondaires, plus fortes que tout. J'avais trop de logique, et toi de sentiment.
> Puis, ils accusèrent le hasard, les circonstances, l'époque où ils étaient nés. (425–26)

> And they looked back over their lives.
> They had both failed, one to realize his dreams of love, the other to fulfill his dreams of power. What was the reason?
> "Perhaps it's because we didn't steer a straight course," said Frédéric.
> "That may be true in your case. But I, on the contrary, was far too rigid in my line of conduct, and I failed to take into account a thousand-and-one minor factors which were really all-important. I was too logical and you were too sentimental."
> Then they blamed chance, circumstances, the times into which they were born. (417–18)

The narrator reports their superficial efforts at explanation in their own words and represents their exterior excuses in a curt summary. The summary keeps the typical novelistic forces—social powers, individuals, chance—in the background. Abandoning such an inquiry for the less troubling task of reminiscence, they fall on the mutual adventure at a brothel in Nogent. The visit, which is told by the narrator, ends when Frédéric's bouquet and lack of presence make the prostitutes laugh, which, in turn, sends the adventurers fleeing. Yet the failure does not diminish their joy. They are happy to be the material of a narrative, for they find that life can be put into a *récit* more easily than novelistic plots can be acted on in life. The coherence of narrative and its signifying structures remain the sources of value, but memory is more pliable material than is reality for uniting narrative and life. Yet this is not enough. They must still use narrative to justify their lives, and for that they need to interpret the story. The characters perform this in their own words:

> Ils se la contèrent prolixement, chacun complétant les souvenirs de l'autre; et, quand ils eurent fini:
> ——C'est là ce que nous avons eu de meilleur! dit Frédéric.
> ——Oui, peut-être bien? C'est là ce que nous avons eu de meilleur! dit Deslauriers. (427)

> They told one another the story at great length, each supplementing the other's recollections; and when they had finished:
> "That was the happiest time we ever had," said Frédéric.
> "Yes, perhaps you're right. That was the happiest time we ever had," said Deslauriers. (419)

The rich thematic implications of the material that Frédéric turns into a redeeming narrative (prostitution, the hero's illusions, his paralyzing fear, and his failure) lead Victor Brombert to call this incident a "retrospective prolepsis of the very essence of the novel" (128), an incident that is consistent with the "metaphoric unity" (130) that he finds in the text. However, to read in this way is to read the text as Frédéric reads his life. Of course, the same themes are present throughout the novel; but the text exposes the incoherence of these codes, opens gaps in them that cannot be closed by a symbolic incident. Moreover, this unifying incident contradicts the one that Frédéric and Mme Arnoux invent in the preceding scene. The facility with which Frédéric creates unifying narratives and redemptive events parodies the realistic assumption that language can reflect and extract the meaning of life. Furthermore, the hero's reading of his life is immediately turned into a cliché by Deslauriers, who repeats Frédéric's judgment word for word. Communication is reduced to the parroting of the same phrases, to the repetition of signifiers. (In *Bouvard et Pécuchet*, mimesis is reduced to copying signifiers.) Thus, Deslauriers's repetition does not signify his agreement or even just the annihilation of differences; it shows how language becomes an object, how its powers of signification dim precisely when the characters feel most confident in using it to order their lives.

Hence, *L'Education* abandons the positivist assumption that links language, perception, and knowledge and changes the problematic of the realistic novel. The project of the novel is no longer to depict the manners of society but to represent the ontological discontinuity of experience, to explore the uncertainties of language's powers of signification and reference. The novel must articulate the paradox of subjectivity, a paradox in which subject is condemned to create the world and name itself, while it (the subject) is immersed in received ideas. This problematic is the bridge to *The Golden Bowl*. Few novels are as different as these two texts in their subject matter and values. However, *L'Education*'s irrealization of the discourse of realism is precisely the opening that James's novels also take in the passage from the middle to the Major Phase.

Part Two
Henry James

5
Setting: Realism Bracketed

IN order to discuss *The Golden Bowl*, we need to break out of the standard reading of the Major Phase, which James's own criticism frequently suggests. This reading tells us that these novels move away from the depiction of the social and physical environment through third-person narration—what I am calling setting—and focus on the "point of view" of individual characters. James's criticism from "The Art of Fiction" (1884) to the Prefaces to the New York Edition (1907–9) employs this vocabulary of perception (e.g., "impression") and consciousness. Perhaps the most influential passage for the reading of James's fiction is the discussion of the "house of fiction" in the Preface to *The Portrait of a Lady*, a house that has "not one window but a million." In each of these windows stands an isolated subject who looks out onto reality:

> But they [the windows] have this mark of their own that at each one of them stands a figure with a pair of eyes, or at least with a field-glass, which forms, again and again, for observation, a unique instrument, insuring to the person making use of it an impression distinct from every other. He and his neighbors are watching the same show, but one seeing more where the other sees less, one seeing black where the other sees

white, one seeing big where the other sees small, one seeing coarse where the other sees fine.[1]

In this passage the subject is isolated from others, and the world is posited as a monolith that differs from the point of view of each subject. We are close to the solipsism of Hume or Berkeley here, and the word "impression" seems to be used much like Locke's notion of a private idea that arises from sense data. (James even defines a novel as "a direct impression of life."[2]) It is not surprising that James criticism has interpreted the word in this way since *The Princeton Encyclopedia of Poetry and Poetics* gives a definition of "image" that comes right out of British empiricism: "an image is a reproduction in the mind of a sensation produced by a physical perception."[3] This model is reinforced by James's discussion of the importance of consciousness. In the Preface to *Roderick Hudson*, we read, "The centre of interest throughout 'Roderick' is in Rowland Mallet's consciousness, and the drama is the very drama of that consciousness" (*AN*, 16). In the Preface to *What Maisie Knew*, we find that Maisie's "small expanding consciousness would have . . . to become presentable as a register of impressions" (*AN*, 142). No less a critic than Fredric Jameson follows the reading suggested by James's vocabulary: [James] "is still theoretically locked into nonsymbolic, essentially 'expressive' categories. For him, the point of view is still a psychological matter of consciousness; but the discovery of the symbolic in its widest sense (all the way from Saussure to semiotics, or from Wittgenstein to Whorf on the one hand and Derrida on the other) is the sheerest repudiation of just such notions as 'consciousness' and 'psychology.' "[4] By examining *The Golden Bowl* in terms of language and reference, we can free the text from this psychologism and empiricism and bring it into a dialogue with contemporary criticism.

The text has many features of realistic discourse that ground the action in London society of approximately 1900. There is no suggestion of the supernatural nor does the symbolism invite the reader to see the characters only as allegorical tags.[5] The most obvious referential force is the use of historical place names: "London," "Brighton," "Paris," "Rome." Moreover, the narrator unambiguously situates the characters in their environments: "He [the Prince] had strayed, simply enough into Bond St. . . ." (I, 3); "Adam Verver at Fawns, that autumn Sunday, might have been observed to open the door of his billiard-room" (I, 125); "The Prince was in his 'own' room, where he often sat now alone; half a dozen open newspapers, the *Figaro* notably, as well as the *Times* were scattered about him" (II, 337).

Despite this realistic grounding, the setting is unlike that of *Les Illusions perdues* or *L'Education*.[6] In James's text, the physical world appears, but it does not impose itself on the characters. "London" does not assert itself as an independent force that stands apart from the characters and influences their actions in the way "Paris" does for the characters in Flaubert and Balzac. Since "London" is primarily a referential marker with an unspecified signification, it can become part of the private vocabulary of the characters or the narrator and take on diverse significations: "The Prince had always liked his London, when it had come to him" (I, 3). The effect of this violation of realistic discourse is heightened by the fact that this sentence is the first of the novel. In the beginning of the realistic novel—or any novel—the reader is given instructions for how to read; and in *L'Education* and *Les Illusions*, the reader finds an extensive description of the cadre that mitigates the semantic voids of proper names and deviant language. When the Prince and Charlotte go on their shopping excursion, we read, "The Prince in especial wondered at his friend's possession of her London. He had rather prized his own possession" (I, 99).

Moreover, there are no historical dates in the text or parallel histories (e.g., the 1848 Revolution in *L'Education*) or references to contemporary historical figures. The absence of historical and physical presence of reality in *The Golden Bowl*—the known—is made verisimilar by having the action take place primarily in private homes (Fawns, Portland Place, Cadogan Place, and Eaton Square), sites that are given proper names and that resist the forces of society. In addition, the action of the novel is limited to six characters, all of whom are concerned with a single problem: the relationships among the four protagonists. That is, not only does the narrator avoid references to the outside world and to public knowledge, but the characters themselves do likewise. We never read what the characters think about theater, politics, or literature. Nor do characters have social ambitions such as Lucien's desire to be a successful writer. Thus, their thoughts and feelings are not "socialized," articulated in the public, intersubjective language of realistic discourse that gives the reader a framework in which she can place the characters' individuality.

"L'effet de réel" of *The Golden Bowl* is achieved not just by the kind of information that the reader receives about the "world" but also by the narrative instance. In *L'Education* the narrator invokes all the forces of "disengagement"[7] when creating physical space. He makes no reference to the act of enunciation through the use of the first or second person, of adverbs that refer to the time of the utterance or of other deictics. This effacement of the narrator's presence maximizes the objectivity of his statements, of the representation. As Edouard Morot-Sir says, "disengagement [*débrayage*] is the antideictic, anti-performative operation *par excellence*. It attempts to separate the referential force from the illocutionary force of language."[8] Flaubert's narrator trifles with this referential force only when he speaks of his characters' thoughts and perceptions or of their sociological components.

James's narrator violates this convention of realistic discourse by speaking in the first person, by addressing the reader directly, by uniting himself with reader ("we"), by identifying his "now" with the represented "now," and by employing other deictics such as demonstratives: "at the moment we are concerned with him" (I, 3); "at present" (I, 19); "as I have said" (I, 19); "she hadn't wished till now" (II, 3–4); "he often sat now alone" (II, 337). The effect of these forces of "engagement" is to problematize both the signification of the referents and the referents themselves. A. J. Greimas defines the effect: "Contrary to what happens at the moment of disengagement, the effect of which is to referentialize the domain where its operation begins, engagement produces a dereferentialization of the utterance that it concerns."[9] We see the narrator struggling for a personal vocabulary to create his narrative rather than relying on the conventions of realistic discourse that permit the narrative to tell itself. Moreover, the referents of the narrator's discourse are not simply the visible world of objects but the invisible world of qualities. As Seymour Chatman says, "thus instead of reference to a thing, which is more or less incidentally qualified, the reader is asked to focus on its quality, that is the quality itself become a thing." For example, instead of "flat statement," we read "flatness of statement."[10] The significance of people and things is not grounded in their physical existence or in their literal "common sensical" meanings as in realistic discourse but in the assertions and agreements of the individual speakers.

Thus, not only does "London" appear primarily as an item in the private vocabularies of the characters but the physical appearance of the characters is rarely described denotatively according to the conventions of realism. When such descriptions do appear, the narrator apologizes for them. After indicating how Charlotte's clothing suggests "winds and waves and customhouses," the narrator devalues his designation of her physical appearance: "making use then of clumsy terms of excess, the face was too narrow and too long . . . and her thick hair was, vulgarly speaking, brown" (I, 46).[11] The narrator calls these terms, which are founded on the realistic attitude, not only "vulgar" but "clumsy." It is not that the text avoids "the real world"—realistic discourse—but that such discourse misrepresents. When the Prince is described, the narrator does not give an anatomical description but an evocation of his aura, of the impression he creates, of his value:

> The Prince's dark blue eyes were of the finest and, on occasion, precisely resembled nothing so much as the high windows of a Roman palace, of an historic front by one of the great old designers, thrown open on a feast-day to the golden air. His look itself at such times, suggested an image—that of some very noble personage . . . (I, 42).[12]

The concrete language in the text is not used to fix physical reality but to set up metaphors and analogies that replace the literal meanings without losing referential force.

However, the setting of the realistic novel is composed not only of physical cadre but also a social one. Since the social world of the novel is not established by the narrator's commentary or the presence of secondary characters—e.g., Pellerin, Sénécal, Arnoux in *L'Education*—the primary components of the setting are the major characters as the narrator presents them to the reader. The "background-information" on characters in a realistic novel does not fulfill functions only for the plot or characters. This information also generates setting by showing the historical and sociological forces that operate in the characters. Moreover, a brief treatment of the characters here will prepare my discussion of Maggie's *Bildungsroman* since she struggles to understand the nature of this private society in Volume II. One of the structures of the *Bildungsroman* is the opposition of the hero/heroine's knowledge with that of the narrator and/or the reader.

The protagonists of *The Golden Bowl* are not firmly situated in social and psychological space as are those of Balzac and Flaubert. The narrator of *Les Illusions perdues* links the thoughts and actions of the characters with certain conventional maxims that reassure the reader that the character is readable, that verisimilitude is not being violated. The characters of *The Golden Bowl* are not so unambiguously constituted. The background information that we receive on them is flushed out for the most part in Fanny's and the Colonel's discussion of the Prince and Charlotte. The information is limited to what is essential to the problem. That is, we find that Charlotte was a poor but well-educated American girl, but we do not find out what she read, what were the formative influences on her character. (One can contrast this treatment with extensive exposition of Isabel's background in *The Portrait of a Lady*.) Most important, "facts" do exist independently of language. The Jamesian text is not simply "withholding" information about the characters or their culture; rather, the text dramatizes the articulation of the past. James's famous aversion to exposition, to "telling" as opposed to "showing," is not simply aesthetic. Since characters must represent their own pasts, they are forced to reengage with it and find a language for it. This can be done through dialogues, such as those between Strether and Maria in *The Ambassadors* or through dramatic interior monologue, as we find in the chapter on Adam Verver's past (Book II, chapter 2). When Strether tries to articulate what he is to someone who does not share his assumptions, he starts to lose a grip on his sense of self and his language.[13] Adam, on the other hand, constructs an essentialist narrative that relieves him from anxiety about who he is. Adam's years as a businessman become the story of redemption in which "his years of darkness" (I, 144) and the death of his uncultivated wife make "possible the years of light" (I, 144) and guide him in the greatest role, "Patron of Art" (I, 150). This story tells us more about Adam's present than the details of his past—his smugness, his vocabulary of acquisition, his affected innocence, etc.

One way the characters and the narrator deal with historical and cultural material is to refer to it as a block of known information. That is, the characters make demands on each other that are like the demands that the text makes on the reader. The reader is assumed to know literary and cultural intertexts on which the novel can draw. In the following passage, for example, we are asked to supply a definition of the real: "They [Maggie and Adam] were avoiding the serious, standing off anxiously from the real..." (II, 257). The Prince's past is designated by the long history of his family that sits in the British Museum, a history to which the characters refer but never enter. This opposition between the known, the unspeakably obvious, and the unknown is one frequently employed. The known is the familiar territory of realistic intertexts, a territory that is cited, devalued and epistemologically undermined by *The Golden Bowl*. The Prince uses this opposition to characterize his two parts. The known is the part that is written up in history books in libraries, while the other part is his " 'single self' " (I, 9). However, the Prince's facile formula does not contain his shifts of identity, and the narrator openly mocks the Prince's reasoning.[14] Knowledge in this text is not something that the narrator, the characters or the reader can stand above and map out in an authoritarian language as in Balzac. The effort to mark out, quantify and disregard the prosaic known is the complement to the notoriously abstract and obscure language that explores the unknown. Thus, the values of the text join those of the characters, as James articulates them in the preface to *The American*:

> The real represents to my perception the things we cannot possibly *not* know, sooner or later, in one way or another; it being but one of the accidents of our hampered state, and one of the incidents of their quantity and number, that particular instances have not yet come our way. The romantic stands, on the other hand, for the things that, with all the facilities in the world, all the wealth and all the courage and all the wit and all the adventure, we can never directly know; the things that can reach us only through the beautiful circuit and subterfuge of our thought and our desire. (*AN*, 31–32)

Thus, the romantic is not opposed to reference or truth-value but merely opposed to the clichés that are in general circulation. The locus of the known in the text is frequently the "ficelle," a character who draws out the main characters—Fanny Assingham here and Maria Gostrey in *The Ambassadors*. These characters have at their disposal the social categories—Balzac's types—as well as particular information that is not available to the protagonist—e.g., Fanny's of Charlotte and the Prince; Maria's of Mme de Vionnet. Unlike Balzac's initiators who give long speeches about the nature of society—who display what they know for the protagonist and the reader—their knowledge is simply referred to, named, rather than displayed. Hence, we read that Maria has "a hundred cases or categories, receptacles of the mind, subdivisions for convenience, in which she pigeon-holed her fellow mortals . . ." (21).[15] The protagonists transcend the categories of social knowledge that the narrator, the other characters, and the reader use to understand them. As Maggie says near the end of the novel, " 'I do *feel*, however, beyond everything—and as a consequence of that, I daresay,' she added with a turn of gaiety, 'seem not to know *where* I am" (II, 263). Knowledge is the tentative effort to figure the pressure of interior and exterior reality, to constitute both the subject and the object, by unleashing all the metaphoric power of language. For example, when the Ververs entertain, we do not "see" conversation among the guests, but Maggie's attempts to create a space for representation through her figures:

> ... Maggie grew to think again of this large element of "company" as of a kind of renewed water supply for the tank in which, like a party of panting gold-fish, they kept afloat.... They learned to live in the perfunctory; they remained in it as many hours of the day as might be; it took on finally the likeness of some spacious central chamber in a haunted house, a great overarched and overglazed rotunda where gaiety might reign, but the doors of which opened into sinister circular passages. (II, 288)

Yet two related questions emerge from these textual strategies. First, do James and his characters try to reinstitute the distinction between public and private socio-linguistic space that Flaubert undoes? Secondly, does James duplicate the tactics that his upper-class characters employ to exile historical and social forces? The answer to the first question is clearly no. The subject does not control a private language—a possibility that Wittgenstein lucidly attacks in the *Philosophical Investigations*—but emerges through linguistic practices. The Ververs' failed efforts to carve out a private world free from manipulation thematize how power, desire, and language cannot be extracted from history. Nonetheless, even if the text unmasks the innocence and aestheticism of the Ververs,[16] James does not address the complicity of his own narrative with the class he represents. Showing how the vocabulary of acquisition, for example, permeates the language and ethics of former businessmen does not adequately represent forces that occupy considerable space in the works of Balzac and Flaubert. However, discussing the Jamesian displacement of economics would lead to a discussion of the text's "political unconscious," which is outside our scope.

Therefore, the concept of setting in realism is intimately bound up with the issue of language and reference. In Balzac's text, the physical and social environments are designated as extralinguistic objects that assert themselves as independent forces; however, these forces are mastered by the meanings proffered by the narrator and the informed characters. In *L'Education*, signification never closes off the referential force. The characters and objects of the text exceed the referential power of realistic discourse. Realistic discourse (clichés) move "laterally" through the minds of the characters without gaining referential authority. In James, the characters and their social space also exceed the meanings offered by the narrator and the characters. Unlike *L'Education*, however, the language of the text is not caught in public discourse. If *L'Education* deprives realistic discourse of its referential authority by exposing the inadequacies of this language in representing subjectivity and objectivity, *The Golden Bowl* merely points toward the limited value of such discourse. James's text explores language's power to mediate and constitute subjective and referential forces. Neither the subject nor the object nor the language that constitutes these two poles is fixed.

6
Speech and Knowledge: The Discovery of New Referential Languages

"To 'put' things is very exactly and responsibly and interminably to do them."[1]
—Henry James

THE problems of language, representation and knowledge haunt the tales of the 1890s. These works foreground metaphysical problems that James's earlier works resolve by presupposition. Tzvetan Todorov in his fascinating article on James's short stories, "Le Secret du récit," maintains that "the secret of the Jamesian narrative is the existence of an essential secret, of an unnamed thing, of an absent and overpowering force that puts the whole narrative machine in motion. The Jamesian movement is double and apparently contradictory (which permits it to begin again ceaselessly): on the one hand, the narrative deploys all its forces to attain a hidden essence, to unveil a secret object; on the other hand, it distances this secret ceaselessly, protects it until the end of the story—if not beyond."[2]

I would recast this idea in philosophical rather than in narratological terms. The secret is not a Proustian essence but a hole in the metaphysics of substance, of realism. The late novels, and in particular *The Golden Bowl*, do not isolate the "secret" but dramatize the creation of referents and secrets. If some of the tales are organized around the search for an ineffable "something" that seems to exist outside the quotidien, *The Golden Bowl* operates on the dialectic between the generation of a "what," a referent, and the speculative reverie on the nature and consequences of the existence of this entity. Neither the characters nor the situation exists before their naming. The "secret" in both *The Ambassadors* and *The Golden Bowl* is a rather banal fact (the sexual component of Chad's relationship with Mme de Vionnet and Charlotte's liaison with the Prince) that is known to the reader and to most of the characters. (In *The Ambassadors*, everyone knows but Strether; in *The Golden Bowl*, Maggie knows that there is "something" between the Prince and Charlotte by the beginning of Volume II.) In both novels, the nature of these "facts" is at issue. When Strether discovers Chad and Mme de Vionnet on the boat, "what" he finds is not what he would have found at the beginning of the novel. All of Volume II shows Maggie's reflections on the nature of her situation and her efforts to change it.

The ambiguous and abstract nature of the text has led critics to read the novel as if it were concerned with peripheral, subtle emotions and stylistic effects, concerns that exile "central" human emotions and issues. William James sums up this view in a letter to Henry shortly after the publication of *The Golden Bowl*:

> You can't skip a word if you are to get the effect, and 19 out 20 worthy readers grow intolerant. The method seems perverse: "Say it *out*, for God's sake," they cry, "and have done with it." And so I say now give us *one* thing in your older director manner, just to show that, in spite of your paradoxical success in this unheard of method, you *can* still write according to accepted canons. Give us that interlude; and then continue like the "curiosity of literature" which you have become. For gleams and innuendoes and felicitous verbal insinuations you are unapproachable, but the *core* of literature is solid. Give it to us *once* again![3]

In the quote from the outraged readers, the pronoun "it" stands for an entity that exists independently of language, an entity that could be discussed "clearly" in another language. William assumes that the "fundamental" matters of literature (life) are easy to articulate and that Henry's language deals with the marginal. This chapter explores the intimate connection of language and knowledge.

In *The Golden Bowl*, Fanny Assingham knows the "facts" about the couple in question, but in this text facts do not compose knowledge. The Prince comes to her at the beginning of the novel and asks for her guidance in dealing with his wife and father-in-law, both of whom speak a language that he cannot grasp. (We know that for Amerigo "the state of mind of his new friends, including Mrs. Assingham herself, had resemblance to a great white curtain" [I,

22].) In response, Fanny cries, " 'What on earth are you talking about?' " (I, 30). Fanny may know certain facts, but she recognizes that these are never enough, and so she tests out metaphorical readings of the principals with the Colonel. These conversations are often comic parodies of the conversations among the main characters. Even though the Assinghams' conversations are comic, they illustrate the way that speech gropes to establish the existence and meaning of its objects. This fluidity at the level of signification and reference manifests itself in various ways in the dialogues; however, I shall limit myself to two sequences of dialogue from Volume I: the discussions between Fanny and the Colonel and those between Charlotte and the Prince. The relative simplicity of these exchanges—in comparison with those in Volume II—will minimize interpretive questions and put the problems of language into relief.[4]

Despite Fanny's obscurity, the Colonel is able to conform to the conventions of conversation without understanding the meaning of the conversation. The narrator tells us early in the novel: "He never went so far as to understand what she meant, and it didn't at all matter, since he could be in spite of the limitation a perfectly social creature" (I, 67). At this point in the novel, Fanny's speculations seem needlessly paranoid, and the reader, who is not fully initiated into the textual processes, tends to sympathize with the Colonel's laconic empiricism and his "realistic" readings of the other characters. This initial sympathy makes the Colonel's later complicity with Fanny powerful. The Colonel tries to be an arbiter who separates knowledge (concepts) from the interesting but epistemologically and ontologically irrelevant "play" of his wife's mind: "He could deal with things perfectly, for all his needs, without getting near them. This was the way he dealt with his wife, a large proportion of whose meanings he could neglect. He edited for their general economy the <u>play</u> of <u>her</u> <u>mind</u>, just as he edited, savingly, with the stump of a pencil, her redundant telegrams" (I, 67). "Mrs. Assingham denied, as we know, that her husband had a <u>play</u> of <u>mind</u>; so that she could on her side, treat these remarks only as if they had been senseless physical gestures or nervous facile movements" (I, 68). Thus, the Assinghams maintain a functional level of intersubjectivity between their very different selves only by ignoring much of the language used to represent these selves and the exterior world. Indeed, at certain moments, Fanny experiences such a distance from her husband that she almost feels as if she is talking to herself: "He made her, when they were together, talk, but as if for some other person; who was in fact for the most part herself." Nonetheless, his presence helps to break the confinement of monologue: "Yet she addressed herself with him as she could never have done without him" (I, 278).

At the end of Volume I Fanny and the Colonel discuss the "situation." Fanny makes an assertion based on her perception: " 'I *see* the boat they're in, but I'm not, thank God, in it myself. Today, however,' Mrs. Assingham added, 'today in Eaton Square I did see' " (I, 370). But the Colonel refuses to put an object after "see"—"see" is often left hovering between transitivity and intransitivity in this text, since objects are not named—and asks the simple and most devastating question, the question that informs the text: " 'Well then what?' " (I, 370). This question sends Fanny scrambling: " 'Oh, many things. More somehow, than ever before. It was as if, God help me, I was seeing *for* them—I mean for the others. It was as if something had happened—I don't know what, except some effect of these days with them at that place—that had either made things come out or had cleared my own eyes' " (I, 370). When Fanny starts to cry, the Colonel seeks to comfort her by agreeing; however, before he can agree he must still find out what "it" is: "she must reassure him, he was made to feel, absolutely in her own way. He'd adopt it and conform to it as soon as he should be able to make it out. The only thing was that it took such incalculable twists and turns" (I, 371).

The Colonel thus asks Fanny to satisfy one of Searle's axioms of reference, the axiom of identification: "If a speaker refers to an object, then he identifies or is able on demand to identify that object for the hearer apart from all other objects."[5] Fanny tries to provide an identifying description, but the description fails to locate an object. The object's ontological status is ambiguous. The "many things" is an impulsive delaying tactic with little referential weight. Then the object is located in another world, a fictional "as if" world. However, the object is not a clearly identifiable object even there, for it becomes an effect, an effect that is generally diffused across space and time ("the few days") and that is so extraordinary that it exists (has meaning) only on "<u>these</u> days" and at "<u>that</u> place." The effect then becomes a cause that operates *either* on the exterior world ("things") or on her cognition ("cleared eyes").

The Colonel, whose literal mindedness provides a contrast to the "things" that Fanny sees, is caught up in the metaphoric process by consenting to talk about these things, by giving them existence. He then loses the firm empirical criteria that he uses to define himself and others. When the Colonel announces his judgment on Charlotte and the Prince earlier in the novel (Book III, Chapter 3) he watches

Fanny take over the meaning of his sentence and paralyze the surrounding semantic field that would permit him to paraphrase this statement or criticize hers. All he has left are the words themselves.

> "They'll manage in their own way," the Colonel almost cryptically repeated.
> It had its effect for her. . . . "So cleverly—*that's* your idea?—that no one will be the wiser? It's your idea that we shall have done all that's required of us if we simply protect them?"
> The Colonel, still in his place, declined however to be drawn into a statement of his idea. Statements were too much like theories, in which one lost one's way; he only knew what he said, and what he said represented the limited vibration of which his confirmed old toughness had been capable. Still, none the less, he had his point to make—for which he took another instant. But he made it for the third time in the same fashion. "They'll manage in their own way." With which he got out. (I, 285–86)

This fluid, negotiable nature of reference and signification leads the characters into agreements—agreements that are not controlled by conscious intentions—that deform the ordinary meanings of words. In the following example the Assinghams discuss Charlotte and the Prince:

> "I think there's nothing they're not now capable of—in their so intense good faith."
> "Good faith?"—he echoed the words, which had in fact something of an odd ring, critically.
> "Their false position. It comes to the same thing." And she bore down with her decision the superficial lack of sequence. "They may very possibly, for a <u>demonstration</u>—as I see them—not have come back." (I, 376–77)

The Assinghams not only negotiate the meaning of words but the existence of events, a negotiation the Colonel assents to only by the repetition of the same words, for he cannot translate them into another statement. He can no longer ignore or edit "the play of her mind." He must put his signature on a statement that he cannot fathom and open himself to possibilities that he had previously dismissed as his wife's fantasies:

> "Nothing—in spite of everything—*will* happen. Nothing *has* happened. Nothing *is* happening."
>
> He looked a trifle disappointed. "I see. For *us*."
>
> "For us. For whom else?" And he was to feel indeed how she wished him to understand it. "We know nothing on earth—!" It was an undertaking he must sign.
>
> So he wrote, as it were, his name. "We know nothing on earth." It was like the soldiers' watchword at night. (I, 400)

The Colonel's signature has wide-reaching implications for the analysis of textual processes. First, it blurs the distinction between constative and performative utterances—that is, between statements that describe a state of affairs and statements that perform an action (e.g., "I promise").[6] Fanny's assertion is a constative utterance *par excellence*. The Colonel's word for word repetition is not simply an "emphatic affirmation"—in Norrman's formula—a successful performative of agreement ("I agree"); it is also a proposition and a double citation. That is, the Colonel uses Fanny's words—the text does not put them in double quotes—to make an assertion of his own about the world. If he were only to mention them, Fanny would not be satisfied. At the same time, the Colonel also mentions Fanny's words since he does not translate her statement into another statement with the same meaning and reference or simply say, "Yes." The words are thus suspended between reflexive, vertical, nonreferential and playful movement and a serious, referential use. The context, the guardian of meaning for speech-act theory, threatens to break down and become part of an unnamed larger context.[7] But the Colonel not only cites Fanny, he cites himself. That is, he repeats the sign of his identity, his presence, his uniqueness in a statement that is not his. (By itself, the signature has deconstructive force, as Derrida points out: "In order to function, that is, in order to be legible, a signature must have a repeatable, iterable, imitable form; it must be able to detach itself from the present and singular intention of its production. It is its sameness, which, in altering its identity and singularity, divides the seal" [*Margins*, 328–29].) By signing, the Colonel can thus appropriate the statement without understanding it, without establishing his presence. To respond to a statement by mentioning the words of the statement is a more disruptive challenge to what is being asserted than the suggestion of an objection or an alternative. The citation of the statement calls the frame, the context, of the statement into question without designating any particular problem in the internal coherence of the statement or in its referential validity. Moreover, by repeating Fanny's words, the Colonel makes a commitment to find his way from his old self to a new self that can understand what "he" has just uttered.

The problems of language and reference that emerge in the Assinghams' dialogues are developed in the scenes between Charlotte and the Prince in Volume I. Charlotte, the mistress of languages, is the most aggressive manipulator of the referential power of language. After coercing the Prince into going on the excursion to buy a present for Maggie, she plays on her impoverished state and makes the Prince agree to keep their outing a secret from Maggie and to listen to her declaration. We read the effect of her persuasion in the narration and free indirect discourse used to represent the Prince's consciousness: "He marked as he could, by this concession, that if he had finally met her first proposal for what would be 'amusing' in it, so any idea she might have would continue to that effect. He had as a consequence—in all consistency—to take it as amusing that she reaffirmed, and reaffirmed again, the truth that was *her* truth" (I, 96). "Truth" in this text is not used to designate a universal proposition but an assertion by an individual or group, an assertion that the narrator does not contradict by proposing an objective language. ("Truth" appears in the first and last sentences of the novel.) However, the proposition that Charlotte offers is strangely lacking in content. She declares that this meeting before his marriage is all she wants. The narrator calls her speech, which is one of the longest in the novel, a "demonstration" (I, 98), and its use of demonstrative pronouns is extraordinary: " 'This is different. This is what I wanted. This is what I've got. This is what I shall always have. This is what I should have missed . . .' " (I, 97).

The demonstrative "this" points insistently toward the present situation and makes it bear the burden of successive predicates in which she puts her possession in several temporal contexts. "This" is then transformed into an object by "what," though further specification cannot be given. The referential force is directed toward an unnamed, intangible, and evanescent feature of the situation.[8]

When Charlotte turns from the representation of her feelings to statements of what she wants the Prince to *know* and to commentary on her previous speech, she refers only to the words that she has just uttered:

> "I wanted you to understand. I wanted you, that is, to hear. I don't care, I think, whether you understand or not. If I ask nothing of you I don't—I mayn't—ask even so much as that.

What you may think of me—that doesn't in the least matter. What I want is that it shall always be with you—so that you'll never be able quite to get rid of it—that I *did*. I won't say that *you* did—you may make as little of that as you like. But that I was here with you where we are and *as* we are—I am just saying this. Giving myself,.in other words, away—and perfectly willing to do it for nothing. That's all." (I, 97–98)

When the Prince does not respond, Charlotte anticipates a question and answers it: " 'You may want to know what I get by it. But that's my own affair' " (I, 98). Charlotte's reasoning is amazing. She begins by referring to an aspect, a property of the present situation and then turns this unnamed item into an entity with "what" and "it." In the above speech she makes a gesture toward a metalanguage that will translate the series of assertions with "this" and tell the Prince "what" he is to understand and how he is to respond (perlocutionary force). Then she dismisses his comprehension by asking only that "it" remain with him, that it mark his memory, the web of his cognitive apparatus. She separates this "it" from herself and from him so that he is not bound to take "it" in any particular way and yet he cannot deny its existence by attributing "it" entirely to her inventiveness. Charlotte thus creates a referential hook for their moments together, a reference that permits the creation of a text by herself and the Prince, even though at this moment Amerigo resists her referential language.[9] The dialogue is a *mise en abyme* of the fundamental dialectic of the text, the dialectic between the establishment of a referent and the reflection on the nature of this entity. The narrator or characters bring "things" into existence by pointing toward them, referring to them and then those entities become points of contention for the characters in dialogue or nodes for their speculative reveries in isolation (next chapter). The characters' generation of their own text[10] is part of the novel's effacement of the differences between life and art, between factual or realistic discourse and imaginative and metaphoric discourse. Moreover, the narrator does not preempt Charlotte's initiative by undermining the existence of the referent or by telling us what it "really" is: "He was glad when finally—the point she had wished to make seeming established to her satisfaction—they brought to what might pass for a close the moment of his life at which he had had least to say" (I, 98).

The text thus departs from traditional conceptions of pronouns and reference. In his study of Nathalie Sarraute, Edouard Morot-Sir describes the effect of this liberation of pronouns from nouns. James,

The Discovery of New Referential Languages   89

like Sarraute, rejects "the implicit ontology of grammars and linguistics according to which pronomination is based on nomination in so far as it presupposes the existence of beings nameable individually and by categories." Thus, "pronouns are no longer subject to the dictatorship of nouns; on the contrary, they serve to break the substantialist envelope that encloses and defines nouns."[11] This use of pronouns also violates Searle's first axiom of reference: "whatever is referred to must exist" (*Speech Acts*, 77). The pronouns in this dialogue function like proper names, not common names. First, they point toward a unique entity, an entity that is outside the language of the other characters. (See Searle's discussion of Frege's "The Thought," *Speech Acts*, 168–69.) Further, even though proper names are not without "sense" (Frege's *Sinn*), they are not the equivalent of definite descriptions:

> But the uniqueness and immense pragmatic convenience of proper names in our language lies precisely in the fact that they enable us to refer publicly to objects without being forced to raise issues and come to an agreement as to which descriptive characteristics exactly constitute the identity of the object. They function not as descriptions, but as pegs on which to hang descriptions. Thus the looseness of the criteria for proper names is a necessary condition for isolating the referring function from the describing function of language. (Searle, 172)

The tension between the referring function and the describing function permits Charlotte and the Prince to create their text and is one of the key oppositions in *The Golden Bowl*.

Through its grammar and its deployment of referential forces, the text thus works against substantialist realism. Bertrand Russell describes the link between the grammar of subject and predicate and substance-attribution metaphysics:

> The influence of language on philosophy has, I believe, been profound and almost unrecognized. If we are not to be misled by this influence, it is necessary to become conscious of it, and to ask ourselves deliberately how far it is legitimate. The subject-predicate logic, with the substance-attribute metaphysic, are a case in point. It is doubtful whether either would have been invented by people speaking a non-Aryan language; certainly they do not seem to have arisen in China with Bud-

dhism, which brought Indian philosophy with it. Again, it is natural, to take a different kind of instance, to suppose that a proper name which can be used significantly stands for a single entity; we suppose that there is more or less a consistent being called 'Socrates' because the same name is applied to a series of occurrences which we are led to regard as appearances of this one being. (*Logic and Knowledge*, 330–31)[12]

However, the force of Charlotte's demonstration is enhanced not only by its extraordinary reference but also by the Prince's agreement to keep the excursion a secret from Maggie and by Charlotte's subsequent conversation, in which she separates Maggie and Adam from herself and the Prince: " 'Certainly,' she said, 'such people as you and I are not' " (I, 102). When the Prince introduces the idea of helping the Ververs, Charlotte opposes "we" to "them": " 'Yes, but if we can't help them?' " The Prince consents to the "we" and that is all Charlotte needs:

> "We *can*—we always can. That is," he competently added, "if we care for them. And that's what we're talking about."
> "Yes"—she on the whole assented. "It comes back then to our absolutely refusing to be spoiled."
> "Certainly. But everything," the Prince laughed as they went on—"all your 'decency,' I mean—comes back to that."
> She walked beside him a moment. "It's just what *I* meant," she then reasonably said. (I, 103)

This passage is a test for any theory of descriptions that employs the principle that equivalent descriptions can be substituted for each other. Both interlocutors agree that they are talking about the same "thing"; however, as each one tries to establish his or her language of representation, the reader is made aware that a change in signification changes the reference. The words used to designate this thing will determine what it is. The Prince backs up and builds his assertion about helping on a proposition to which Charlotte must assent, and he makes this proposition the subject of their entire conversation through his use of "that" and "what." However, Charlotte assents by using an ambiguous pronoun herself, "it" (which may or may not be the same as the Prince's "that") and by substituting her own predicate. In the Prince's statement, the two will act for Maggie and Adam, while in Charlotte's restatement they resist the Ververs.

Charlotte's use of reference reemerges in the shop, when the

The Discovery of New Referential Languages 91

Prince offers her a gift, a "ricordo" of "this little hunt" (I, 108). Charlotte resists the offer, saying that his offer runs against her "logic": " 'But logic's everything. That at least is how I feel it. A ricordo from you—from you to me—is a ricordo of nothing. It has no reference!' " (I, 108). When the Prince can answer only, " 'Ah, my dear,' " Charlotte pursues, " 'You don't refer,' she went on to her companion. '*I* refer' " (I, 109).

At this point, Charlotte has a new referential language that excludes the Prince's language, which is still attached to the past and the Ververs. The Prince's language does not refer for Charlotte. A gift—which symbolizes the link between reference to the self and to the exterior world—from the Prince, like the language that he speaks, has no meaning or reference in the semantic system that she wants to establish. All references will be made by Charlotte; she is willing to offer him a gift.

However, when the Prince and Charlotte go into the shop and Charlotte sees the bowl, she loses her control over the signification of the present. The Prince immediately walks out of the store, and she is left to haggle with the owner. Even though she learns from him that the bowl has a flaw, she still likes it and wants to offer it to the Prince (I, 114). He, however, would never accept it because of its flaw. Her willingness to objectify the significance of the situation with a symbol has left her vulnerable to the esthete Prince's judgment. Charlotte starts her retreat with a lie—she tells him the bowl costs five pounds instead of fifteen—and then by her inability to continue the search for a *present* (if I may pun here). Her moments alone with the shopkeeper had "the effect of their having, by some tacit logic, some queer inevitability, quite dropped the idea of a continued pursuit" (I, 117). The halt in the pursuit, in her "demonstration" forces her out of the present into the conditional: " 'You'd be afraid—?' " (I, 119). Charlotte then ventures guesses about what the Prince is afraid of and the Prince repeats her suggestion word for word. He supplies her no more than her own words until he concludes, " 'For everything.' "

The Prince then tries to take the offensive when he shifts the tense to the future and maintains that he will give her a present on the day she marries. Charlotte is up to the occasion, however, and reverses the conditions by making the gift precipitate the marriage instead of the contrary: " 'Well, I would marry, I think, to have something from you in all freedom' " (I, 121).[13]

The power of this common point of reference culminates in the pledge-scene (Book III, Chapters 4 and 5). The chapter begins with the Prince's reflections on Charlotte's earlier conversations; then when she comes to visit him, he recognizes how they are bound together by links, by a text that they did not consciously create: "What happened in short was that Charlotte and he had by a single turn of the wrist of fate—'led up' to indeed, no doubt, by steps and stages that conscious computation had missed—been placed face to face in a freedom that extraordinarily partook of ideal perfection, since the magic web had spun itself without their toil, almost without their touch" (I, 298). (The "almost" helps undermine the innocence of this creation.)

The narrator again calls Charlotte's exchange with the Prince a "demonstration," but it is a demonstration of a peculiarly Jamesian kind: "The whole demonstration, none the less, presented itself as taking place at a very high level of debate—in the cool upper air of the finer discrimination, the deeper sincerity, the larger philosophy. No matter what the facts invoked and arrayed, it was only a question as yet of their seeing their way together" (I, 300–301). The repeated definite article and the false comparative in the above citation invoke a presupposition—finer than what?—on the part of the reader. (*L'Education* makes a similar assumption in the famous line from III, 6: "Il connut la mélancolie des paquebots, les froids réveils sous la tente, l'étourdissement des paysages et des ruines, l'amertume des sympathies interrompues" [419].) The reader like the Prince must follow the argument, which is built on assumptions and assertions about the world (about the existence and meaning of moral "things") and about the Prince's knowledge of these entities. Charlotte begins with an assertion about the Prince's knowledge: " 'You knew, besides, you knew today I would come. And if you knew that you know everything.' " Her next sentence is a proposition about their situation: " 'Above all,' she said, 'there has been the personal romance of it' " (I, 301). When the Prince does not understand, she follows up with another assertion about his knowledge: " 'You can't not know', she said, 'where you are' " (I, 302). In the next step, she again makes a statement about the situation and then uses the statement as a lever for drawing the two of them together: " 'There it all is—extraordinary beyond words. It makes such a relation for us as, I verily believe, was never before in the world thrust upon two well-meaning creatures. Haven't we therefore to take things as we find them?' " (I, 302–3). When the Prince resists, she uses the visit itself as a secret bond—thus, repeating the device of the earlier scene—by asking what the Prince will do if Maggie comes in and then providing him with an answer: " 'It seems to me we must say the same thing' " (I, 308). Finally the Prince agrees to "act in concert," and this agreement provides a context for their closing exchange, in which they repeat, " 'it's too wonderful,' " " 'too beautiful,' " " 'sacred' " (I, 312), in which they do indeed "say the same thing." Again the use of the pronoun enables the speakers to agree on a referent without agreeing on the signification. In the previous scene, word for word repetition was in the interrogative, where the Prince agreed only to the words that Charlotte provided him with. Here the repetition brings about an experience of union. Agreements in this text are so tenuous that they do not permit paraphrase, only the sounding of the same words. Like "it" or "that" that picks out (creates) an entity in the world, spoken words become the referents, become a chant that is an experience of fusion. Once Charlotte and the Prince agree to a common referential language, they establish an intersubjective link that draws them together and separates them from the Ververs. These dialogues offer a passionate dramatization of Heidegger's adage that "Being speaks always and everywhere throughout language."

7
Narrator: Reference and the Language of Being

THE radical discontinuities generated by the Jamesian dialogues puts the narrator in an unusual situation. In chapter 5, I discussed how the narrator violates the enunciative conventions of realism by referring to the narrative instance. However, it is important to note that these violations do not simply point to an ineffable subjectivity; on the contrary, many of the narrator's interventions assure the reader of the reliability of his representation. In this respect, the Jamesian narrator resembles that of Balzac more than the Flaubertian narrator, who teases the reader with clichés and who questions the authority of the realistic discourse that he employs. In a historical context, the Jamesian narrator is in an analogous position to the Balzacian narrator. Balzac's narrator wants to reinforce the establishment of a positivistic realistic discourse and thus feels the need to persuade the reader of the validity of his language. In his article, "Vraisemblance et motivation," Gérard Genette addresses the function of Balzacian commentary: "Its most frequent and characteristic manifestation is the justification of a particular fact with a general law that the reader supposedly does not know or perhaps has forgotten."[1] Since the verisimilitude of a narrative depends on the concordance of the representation with the *idées reçues* of the public, textual violations of these maxims are often accompanied by a new maxim that motivates the represented action.[2]

James's narrator is also offering a language of representation that is outside the conventions of verisimilitude of realistic discourse. Without the narrator's insistence on the referential force of the language, the reader may read the text in a "symbolic" genre and categorize it with the tales of 1890s or he may ascribe the extravagance of the language to the "point of view" of the characters. Unlike the Balzacian narrator, however, the narrator of *The Golden Bowl* intervenes only to make phatic or narratological statements, not to provide motivating maxims. That is, he intervenes only to reassure the reader about the reality and reliability of the representation or to distinguish between his voice and that of the characters. The narrator does not generate maxims even though the text represents feelings that are outside the *idées reçues* that make up the lexicon of realism and that permit "nonnarrated discourse."[3] The text "defamiliarizes," to use the Russian Formalist term, the language of realism that the reader expects in a hackneyed tale of adultery and father/daughter attachment; however, the language cannot be reduced to the Formalist notion of "device." "Jealousy," "love" cannot be applied in their conventional sense as in Balzac. *L'Education* unmasks the inadequacy and arbitrariness of these platitudes, cuts them loose from the interior and exterior life of the characters and opens up an experiential and referential space that language does not fill. *The Golden Bowl* figures this space. In the following passage not only are Maggie's feelings opposed to conventional "jealousy," but the conventional responses that exemplify this word appear as fantastic, metaphoric beings themselves:

> ... she saw as in a picture, with the temptation she had fled from quite extinct, why it was she had been able to give herself from the first so little to the vulgar heat of her wrong. She might fairly ... have yearned for it, for the straight vindictive view, the rights of resentment, the rages of jealousy, the protests of passion, as for something she had been cheated of not least: a range of feelings which for many women would have meant so much, but for *her* husband's wife, for her father's daughter, figured nothing nearer to experience than a wild eastern caravan, looming into view with crude colours in the sun, fierce pipes in the air, high spears against the sky, all a thrill, a natural joy to mingle with, but turning off short before it reached her and plunging into other defiles. (II, 236–37)[4]

The characters' feelings of being "lost" or "at sea" are not just feelings of separation from the other characters but from a language that can make the "situation" and their interior life coherent. "What" has happened or is happening is always the character's experience and not some objective event, and the narrator frequently intervenes to represent this experience through analogies and metaphors that exceed the characters' consciousness and language. These metaphors and comparisons do not simply make literal meanings concrete; they become the space of thought and reverie that englobes the literal, as the preceding quotation on jealousy illustrates. The text thus plays with the distinction between literal and figural in a way that justifies Nietzsche's famous quote on the ubiquity of metaphor:

> What therefore is truth? A mobile army of metaphors, metonymies, anthropomorphisms: in short a sum of human relations which become poetically and rhetorically intensified, metamorphosed, adorned, and after long usage seem to a nation fixed, canonic and binding; truths are illusions of which one has forgotten that they are illusions; worn-out metaphors which have become powerless to affect the senses.[5]

By refusing to subordinate itself to literal meaning metaphor works against the ontology of realism. Like pronouns that assert problematic referents, the figures in the text propose an alternative language for locating reference and meaning. This is not to say that all meanings are figural or that the figural operates independently of the literal. Rather, the dynamic tension between the figural and the literal animates the novel's "general economy" of signification, to use Derrida's phrase.[6] These figures take on enormous importance since the text is not concerned with the characters' actions or even the operations of their consciousness but with the tension among alternative theories of being. The "consciousness" or "mind" of a character is the site for the appearance of a proposition.

The best illustration of the relationships among metaphor, reference, and being is in the beginning of Volume II. At this point, Maggie is contemplating her new insight about the nature of the relationships among the four protagonists and the significance of her own recent action that she used to signal to the Prince and Charlotte her recognition of the change. This is a typical moment in the Jamesian text, the moment in which a character reflects on an action that has not yet been reported. The past incident then appears not simply as a reported action or a typical flashback. (The series of events is not picked up until four pages later and not finished until the next chapter.) These events—like most events in the novel—are dramatized in dialogue or told through someone's consciousness. Almost none of the events is reported in the "objective" aorist.[7] Thus, the narrative structure emphasizes the indeterminacy of the meaning of the actions, the way that significance of events is not something "added" to their objective existence but coextensive with the language of representation. The reader sees "what" the situation is for Maggie through a comparison with a pagoda:

> This situation had been occupying for months and months the very centre of the garden of her life, but it had reared itself there like some strange tall tower of ivory, or perhaps rather some wonderful beautiful but outlandish pagoda.... She had walked round and round it—that was what she felt; she had carried on her existence in the space left her for circulation.... At present however, to her considering mind, it was as if she had ceased merely to circle and to scan the elevation, ceased so vaguely, so quite helplessly to stare and wonder. (II, 3–4)

The narrator emphasizes that he is speaking in his own voice by his announcement at the beginning of the next paragraph: "If this image, however, may represent our young woman's consciousness of a recent change in her life—a change now but a few days old—it must at the same time be observed that she both sought and found in renewed circulation, as I have called it, a measure of relief from the idea of having perhaps to answer for what she had done" (II, 4–5).

The Jamesian and New Critical terminology—"center of consciousness" and "point of view"—does not adequately isolate the nature of the discourse or account for its effect. First, the analogy is the narrator's and not Maggie's; it does not represent only her "consciousness" but her feeling, her unconscious engagement with a change that she cannot imagine.[8] The narrator separates his language from the language of the character: "That in fact may pass as the very picture of her semi-smothered agitation..." (II, 8).[9] (Thus, "consciousness" in the passage "our young woman's consciousness" cited above means subjectivity.) The narrator also signals the passage to Maggie's own thoughts, or more accurately, to free indirect representation of reflective consciousness, with the phrase "as she liked to put it": "The pagoda in her blooming garden figured the arrangement—how otherwise was it to be named?—by which, so strikingly, she had been able to marry without breaking, as she liked to put it, with her past" (II, 5). The passage that follows shows how Maggie consciously conceives of the arrangement before she sees a problem. Even though some of the verbs in the passage represent "actions," the use of the past perfect makes these statements propositions about a state of being. The assertive force necessary to make these propositions cohere is underlined by "moreover." States of affairs can never be passively and objectively named in *The Golden Bowl*. Naming a state of affairs is always an argument:

> She had surrendered herself to her husband without the shadow of a reserve or a condition and yet she hadn't all the while given up her father by the least little inch. She had compassed the high[10] felicity of seeing the two men beautifully take to each other, and nothing in her marriage had marked it as more happy than this fact of its having practically given the elder, the lonelier, a new friend. What had <u>moreover</u> all the while enriched the whole aspect of success was that the latter's marriage had been no more measurably paid for than her own. (II, 5)

This tight little scheme is the way Maggie packages everyone before her recognition; the facility of the scheme is matched by the controlled prose that fits each piece together without resorting to the metaphoric extravagance employed by the narrator. Actions and characters make sense when they are placed in a "system," systems that resolve ambiguity by presupposition rather than by analysis, systems that remove relationships from discord and time—time here is an endlessly repetitive synchronic movement—and knowledge that comes through alienation. By the end of the paragraph, the narrator intervenes and characterizes Maggie's consciousness since she has now become aware of elements for which she has no language:

> So it was that their felicity [the four protagonists or Maggie and Adam] had fructified; so it was that the ivory tower, visible and admirable doubtless from any point of the social field, had risen stage by stage. Maggie's actual reluctance to ask herself with proportionate sharpness why she had ceased to take comfort in the sight of it represented accordingly a lapse from that ideal consistency on which her moral comfort al-

most at any time depended. To remain consistent she had always been capable of cutting down more or less her prior term. (II, 6)

The preceding passages illustrate the way the text's figures develop tensions among alternative theories of being. The pagoda provides a logical space that is independent of the logical space designated by Maggie's literal propositions about the existing state of affairs. The semantic interaction between these different logical spaces—e.g., her feeling of harmony and inclusion in the propositions versus her feelings of strangeness and exclusion in the analogy, the transparency of the meaning of the relationships for all parties versus the hidden chambers and unreadable surface of the pagoda—opens new referential possibilities in the same "state of affairs." The reference of these two opposing spaces is the same. That is, the literal and figural point toward the same "things"—the necessary moment of identification and reification—for example, that Adam, the Prince and Charlotte are the same entities that they were. The analogy suggests potential revelations at the level of signification and reference. Metaphors can illustrate propositions, though they carry a potential challenge to what they illustrate.[11] Thus, figures carry a similar potential for tension between reference and signification as do proper names. The tensions between competing definite descriptions—in the mind of one individual or different ones—and between any definite description and the referential power of the name are similar to those in metaphor and analogy.

The figures in the text thus have the three powers that Roland Barthes finds in proper names and the reminiscence: "the power of essentialization (since the name designates only one referent)"; "the power of citation (since one can call up at will any essence enclosed in the name by proferring it)"; "the power of exploration (since one 'unfolds' a proper name exactly as one does a memory)."[12]

My example may appear to be an unusual case since the narrator is the speaker of this analogy about Maggie's feeling. However, analogies most frequently appear in this text at moments of disruption, when the character's system of understanding collapses. Also, this example is unusual because we are given both the analogy and the literal statements (one page later). In other examples (e.g., the spaniel analogy, II, 6–7), the text does not give as many literal statements. In other places, the reader must rely entirely on context to provide a "literal" ground for the comparison: "It was for hours and hours later on as if she had somehow been lifted aloft, were floated and carried on some warm high tide . . ." (II, 24–25). The narrator's analogies are often a step toward literal statements that can represent what the analogy suggests. Maggie's own analogies (e.g., the carriage, II, 23–24) are an intermediate stage that is followed by her ability to make literal statements and logical plans, as we shall see in the next chapter on character.

Not only does the narrator generate tension among alternative theories of being through analogies, he also backs away from his own language by calling attention to his choice of words, which can be seen in other passages in this section: "if this image, however, may represent our young woman's consciousness" (II, 4): "that in fact may pass as the very picture" (II, 8); "might I so far multiply my metaphors" (II, 7).[13] Like the narrator of *L'Education*, the narrator of *The Golden Bowl* proposes no authoritarian language that embraces all events, refuses to explain and solidify the world of the text in the way that Balzac's narrator does. Actions, appearances, and words take on their meanings from the system, the speech community into which they are inserted. There is no englobing speech community that unites character, narrator and reader as in Balzac. Gaps can emerge between characters, as we saw in the previous chapter, or within characters, as we see in Maggie's divided subjectivity. The powers of signification never exhaust the powers of reference. The text points toward objects (other characters, events, words, feelings) that we and the characters feel but cannot name.

This reading of the narrator's voice and of his use of figures contrasts with the traditional reading of "point of view" and offers a new view of James's place in literary history. Since all the language is typically read as representing Maggie's intentionality, one finds remarks such as F. O. Matthiessen's that "James's novels are strictly novels of intelligence rather than full consciousness."[14] However, if one agrees that the analogies and metaphors are the narrator's and not the characters', then these figures probe more "deeply" than does stream of consciousness, a technique that captures the immediacy of thought but is limited to the character's ability to formulate thoughts. In *Transparent Minds*, Dorrit Cohn distinguishes "interior monologue" and "psycho-narration," where the narrator intervenes in order to represent pre-verbal levels of consciousness. She clarifies the distinction with reference to Robert Musil: "Musil has clearly used a deliberate psycho-analogical method for rendering consciousness in order to avoid interior discourse techniques, and to reach a sub-verbal stratum in his character's mind, 'a life that cannot be expressed in words, and which is my life nonetheless.' "[15]

Another consequence of the conflation of the narrator's and character's voices is that the force of the metaphors is reduced to the character's consciousness, which is opposed to the facts of the world. For example, in Ruth Yeazell's interesting reading of the spaniel metaphor (Yeazell, 41–44, *The Golden Bowl*, II, 6–7) she claims that the metaphor represents Maggie's refusal to engage "the facts": "the language which defines her new awareness remains in the context of metaphor rather than fact" (43). Instead of reading James as a "premodern" or a modern who leads up to interior monologue, we need to take the Major Phase out of the psychology of consciousness and explore the postmodern dimension of the text's dramatization of language and subjectivity.[16]

Thus, the known is not an assemblage of facts but a fluid category into which phenomena enter. After Fanny and the Colonel's emotional dialogue in Book III, Chapter 10, we read: "What was between them had opened out further, had somehow, through the sharp show of her feeling, taken a positive stride, had entered, as it were, without more words, the region of the understood, shutting the door after it and bringing them so still more nearly face to face" (I, 378). A character possesses knowledge in James when he or she operates confidently in a system of assumptions governing the meanings of words and actions. Thus, knowledge does not correspond to an objective truth but to an agreement about meaning. Once a character perceives an incongruity in his interior or exterior world, his knowledge, his collection of literal meanings starts to crumble and he is forced into the figural. (The narrator uses figurative language to represent what is "literal" for the character.) Sometimes the figure brings the dissonant perception into the system without abandoning the system—e.g., Maggie's strategy of "cutting down the prior term" (II, 6); at other times, an entirely new system must be erected in order for the "known" to reestablish itself. We watch Maggie struggle to make such a system in Volume II. This eruption of metaphor in the discourse of realism is reinforced by other stylistic features, many of which have been isolated and analyzed by Seymour Chatman in *The Later Style of Henry James*, a work to which I am greatly indebted even though I do not share Chatman's philosophical presuppositions.[17]

One of the most important features of James's style is nominalization. Chatman discusses the grammatical transformation involved in this structure and its effects:

> To transform 'John observed X' or 'John apparently decided that p' into 'John's observation was X' or 'John's decision ap-

peared to be p' is (regardless of the degree of concreteness of 'X' or 'p') to put on stage an abstract entity where previously there had been only a human actor. When you nominalize such a verb, you are presenting an entity for inspection, an entity capable of undergoing full elaboration and qualification, even of becoming (as not infrequently in James) a complete personification.... Thoughts and perceptions in James's world are entities more than actions, things more than movements. They occupy a space—the mind; though intangible, they are 'things' in the mind. Further, there is established between them and the characters a relation not unlike the relation which characters bear to each other, indeed, one which may be livelier and in some ways more important. (29)

The effect of foregrounding entities at the expense of characters is to upset one of the hallmarks of realism, the unified character who is an agent in the world. Characters are invaded, traversed by pressures from discourse, from feelings and from the exterior world. Characters do not control the interaction of subject and object; "they" are immersed in forces. Thus, the Major Phase does not simply turn from the representation of the exterior world to the representation of consciousness; it asks the reader to abandon the model of subject versus object and to focus on the constitution of subjects and objects, not only on their interaction. Early in Volume II, Maggie waits for the Prince to come down from his bath: "The hour was filled nevertheless with the effect of his nearness, and above all with the effect, strange in an intimacy so established, of an almost renewed vision of the facts of his aspect" (II, 21). Several pages later, a moment of her consciousness is personified: "[T]hat consciousness, lately born in her, had been taught the evening before to accept a temporary lapse, but had quickly enough again, with her getting out of her own house and her walking across half the town—for she had come from Portland Place on foot—found breath still in its lungs" (II, 31). Moreover, language can move the characters: "Once launched, himself [the Prince], at any rate, as he had been directed by all the terms of the intercourse between Portland Place and Eaton Square, once steeped at Matcham in the enjoyment of a splendid hospitality, he found everything, for his interpretation, for his convenience, fall easily enough into place ... (I, 330). "The theory, visibly, had patched itself together for her that the dear woman [Fanny] had somehow from the early time had a hand in *all* their fortunes" (II, 102). These structures do not simply "reflect" the passivity of the Jamesian character; rather, they rewrite the constitution of subjectivity and agency.

Another disruptive force is the use of cleft sentences,[18] which increases the number of nontransitive verbs—copulas, passives, intransitives. Actions become grouped into entities by "what" or "it". These actions do not take place in an ontologically secure world; rather, they are the subjects of existential propositions, propositions whose very formulation questions the nature and the meaning of these actions: "What befell however was that even while she thus waited she felt herself present at a process taking place rather deeper within him . . ." (II, 28). (Without the cleft construction the sentence would read: "However, even while she thus waited . . .") The referential status of the "what" is often problematic: "But what perhaps most came out in the light of these concatenations was that it had been for all the world as if Charlotte had been 'had in' . . ." (II, 23). The "what" ("it") is an intangible object that emerges over time and through the optic of "these concatenations." The nature of this object is specified by the familiar, the known, through the colloquial expression, but this concept operates only by analogy from the "as if" world. The passive ("had been had in") keeps active, causal forces out of sight. The expletive "it" works in a similar way and this structure often appears in the text with an "as if": "It was for hours and hours later on as if she had somehow been lifted aloft, were floated and carried on some warm high tide . . ." (II, 24–25). The verb "was" gives the proposition referential force while the "as if" generates an alternative world, a metaphor. Chatman concludes that the effect of the text's abstraction and non-transitive verbs is to move "away from, not toward, drama. For acts become nominalized, and their predicate is the copula, the verb form for exposition, for a listing of particulars and propositions. Instead of actors performing on a stage, there are increasing numbers of statements of the existence of things" (81). Though Chatman does not expand this statement, his point supports my argument that the text challenges a realistic ontology, an ontology that valorizes a perceptual denominative vocabulary for regulating the interaction of subject and object. In *The Golden Bowl*, characters do not control their subjectivity nor does perception govern objectivity. The text is not concerned with a series of actions within a fixed ontology but with the fluctuation of being that simultaneously produces both subject and object.[19]

In addition, the text plays with two of the principal coordinates of realistic discourse, causality and temporality. In *The Golden Bowl*, causality is not an objective linear chain that ties events together, but is continually refigured by the characters and the narrator: "It had been an hour from which the chain of causes and consequences was definitely traceable—so many things, and at the head of the list her father's marriage, having appeared to her to flow from Charlotte's visit to Fawns, and that event itself having flowed from the memorable talk" (II, 22–23).[20] This linear figure is immediately replaced by a synchronic figure, the carriage, where Charlotte is the fourth wheel, which is then transformed into a coach pulled by the Prince and Charlotte with Maggie and her father inside.[21] The linear metaphor of time is not privileged. Unlike *L'Education* with the narrator's relentless temporal adverbs—"puis", "alors", "et" (logical and temporal gap)—that underline the passage of time, from an exterior point of view, the narrator of *The Golden Bowl* lets the characters give shape to past or future time. When Maggie and Adam are discussing their futures, Maggie wants "to keep him with her for remounting the stream of time and dipping again, for the softness of the water, into the contracted basin of the past" (II, 258). In Volume I, Charlotte suggests the future is an alternately obvious and ambiguous path that she and the Prince must "cut together." These temporally separate suggestions are grouped as a series of alternative propositions:

> There were hours when she spoke of their [Prince and Charlotte] taking refuge in what she called the commonest tact—as if this principle alone would suffice to light their way; there were others when it might have seemed, to listen to her, that their course would demand of them the most anxious study and the most independent, not to say original, interpretation of signs. She talked now as if it were indicated at every turn by finger-posts of almost ridiculous prominence; she talked again as if it lurked in devious ways and were to be tracked through bush and briar; and she even on opportunity delivered herself in the sense that, as their situation was unprecedented, so their heaven was without stars. (I, 288)

Until the Prince comes to an agreement with her (the pledge-scene of Book III, Chapter 5), the circular flow of the present system is a force—with the power of the Ververs behind it—that must be worked against, untracked by the linear path of a "new" future.[22] Thus, we see the dialogues between the two lovers and the long reflections of the Prince. The time of the discourse is frequently greater than the time of the story. Once a system is established the text takes up reflective or iterative narration to characterize an entire period.

Thus, temporal intervals are marked by changes in the situation, changes that are awaited or not (the discovery of the bowl). In addition to the absence of historical dates, there are no firm temporal markers for the chapters—except for the large ellipses—and the use of remembered rather than direct representation permits the narrator to arrange events independently of chronology. Maggie's contemplation takes place "several days" after the events reported in the preceding chapter. The time of the *histoire* does not dictate the time of the *récit*. Nor is time "merely" subjective. The character's experience of time is not entirely under her control. Time dilates or contracts so that even the Colonel, the anxious watcher and waiter, the reader's ficelle, is without temporal bearings:

> His [the Colonel's] present position, clearly, was that of seeing her [Fanny] in the centre of her sheet of dark water, and of wondering if her actual mute gaze at him didn't perhaps mean that her planks *were* now parting. . . . He watched her steadily paddle, always a little nearer, and at last he felt her boat bump. The bump was distinct, and in fact she stepped ashore. "We were all wrong. There's nothing." (I, 366)

A good example of the representation of time and argument is the sequence from Book III, chapters 4, 5, and 6. Chapter 4 takes up Charlotte and the Prince's situation some time after the reception that opens Book III, "a couple of years" (I, 245) after Charlotte's marriage to Adam. (Book III, Chapters 1, 2, and 3, are dialogues between Charlotte and Fanny, Fanny and the Prince, and Fanny and the Colonel, respectively.) The argumentative (rhetorical) nature of time appears in the first line of Book III, 4: "It appeared <u>thus</u> that they might enjoy together extraordinary freedom, the two friends, from <u>the moment</u> they <u>should understand</u> their position aright" (I, 288). Charlotte wants to install this moment into her own and the Prince's sense of time, a moment that can take place only after an agreement. The Prince has not accepted this moment:

> For the Prince himself, meanwhile, time, in its measured allowance, had originally much helped him—helped him in the sense of there not being enough of it to trip him up; in spite of which it was just this accessory element that seemed at present, with wonders of patience, to lie in wait. Time had begotten at first, more than anything else, separations, delays and intervals; but it was troublesomely less of an aid from the

moment it began so to abound that he had to meet the question of what to do with it. (I, 291)

Time is not just experienced by the Prince; it becomes an actor that acts on the characters and that figures as a subject in the textual argument. Time becomes a quantity that fits into the Prince's equation: "And there was a logic in the matter, he knew; a logic that but gave this truth a sort of solidity of evidence" (I, 292). It is noteworthy that in this Jamesian reasoning "logic" is relativized by "a" and that the normal relationship of truth and evidence is reversed. Usually, evidence leads up to truth; here, truth moves toward evidence.

The narrator then moves from these undated reflections to a particular moment, on "one dark day on which, by an odd but not unprecedented chance, the reflexions just noted offered themselves as his main recreation" (I, 293–94). Charlotte then appears "at the very climax of his special inner vision" (I, 295). The result is that past and future lock in an embrace—obviously anticipating the embrace that is to come—an embrace that squeezes out the present: "The sense of the past revived for him nevertheless as it hadn't yet done: it made that other time somehow meet the future close, interlocking with it, before his watching eyes, as in a long embrace of arms and lips, and so handling and hustling the present that this poor quantity scarce retained substance enough, scarce remained sufficiently *there*, to be wounded or shocked" (I, 297–98). Time as an actor must, of course, be distinguished from experienced time, on which the text is focusing with increasing intensity at this point. In Book III, 5, the present is represented in dialogue, in which Charlotte makes a demonstration to which the Prince agrees. However, the force of his agreement does not end with their embrace; it reverberates through his principles. Book III, 6, opens with argument and time united again: "He had taken it from her, as we have seen moreover, that Fanny Assingham didn't now matter—the 'now' he had even himself supplied, as no more than fair to his sense of various earlier stages" (I, 313). The Prince accepts Charlotte's statement about Fanny's exile and then makes a place for this statement in his representation of Fanny. He consigns Fanny's resistance to his liaison with Charlotte to her (Fanny's) failure of wit (I, 314), a characteristic she shares with the Ververs, and then makes this failure something new so he can explain those moments of understanding that he previously felt with Fanny ("various earlier stages"). The text then moves into the iterative representation of the new system that his agreement has brought into being (I, 315), a representation that the narrator condenses, orders and situates: "Well, that Charlotte might be appraised as at last not ineffectually recognising it was a reflexion that, during the days with which we are actually engaged, completed in the Prince's breast these others, these images and ruminations of his leisure, these gropings and fittings of his conscience and his experience, that we have attempted to set in order here" (I, 319). The Prince is working out the consequences of his agreement and emerges with a conclusion—represented in FID—that he must stop being Adam's constant companion: "To haunt Eaton Square in fine would be to show that he hadn't, like his brilliant associate, a sufficiency of work in the world" (I, 320).

The subsequent narration of the Ververs' Easter party develops the particulars of these speculations. The linear movement of time is thus subordinated to the typical reflections of a period of time. This is not just, to use James's own words, a technique "of composition, of foreshortening, of the proportion and relation of parts."[23] This represents the character's experience of time and the text's own movement of consolidation. That is, the text is organized around reference. In some cases, we see a drama of constitution—e.g., Maggie's meditation at the beginning of Volume II. At other moments, we see the effect of the new referent as it reorients a character's imagination, as we just saw with the Prince.[24]

The next chapter opens with a shift in the temporal and argumentative forces: "The main interest of these hours [at the party] for us, however, will have been in the way the Prince continued to know, during a particular succession of others, separated from the evening in Eaton Square by a short interval, a certain persistent aftertaste" (I, 326). The Prince will encounter a complication ("Something had rather momentously occurred, in Eaton Square, during his enjoyed minutes with his old friend [Fanny]," [I, 328]), and time shifts from the iterative to the singulative.

Nevertheless, the event becomes the source for more speculation, for more imaginative play: "[B]ut whatever the object he just now fingered it a good deal out of sight—amounting as it mainly did for him to a restless play of memory and a fine embroidery of thought" (I, 328). The word "play," which recurs many times in the text, has a distinctly Kantian sense, which the following quotations will make clear: "The play of vision was at all events so rooted in him [Adam] that he could receive impressions of sense even while positively thinking" (I, 188); "This backward speculation, had it begun to play, however, would have been easily arrested" (I, 323); ". . . a spirit that positively played with the facts" (I, 353); "Such things, as I say, were to come back to her—they played through her full after-sense like lights on the whole impression . . ." (II, 20).[25]

The evocation of Kantian aesthetics gives insight into the values at work in the textual imagination. For Kant, an aesthetic judgment is founded on "the feeling (of internal sense) of that harmony in the play of the mental powers, so far as it can be felt in sensation."[26] Kant isolates aesthetic judgments from knowledge and ethics, which he addresses in his other critiques. In James's novel, however, aesthetic play of semantic resemblance and difference expands the horizon of referential and ethical values.[27] At the same time, however, the text dramatizes the dangers of aesthetic play that becomes detached from the values of goodness and truth. The novel criticizes detached, self-satisfied aestheticism (particularly in the Prince and Adam) and shows how this detachment lends itself to appropriation by other values. Aesthetic play seeks harmony independently of truth and goodness. Adam's union of aesthetic play and acquisition and the Prince's reduction of people and things to objects of amusement are the two most obvious examples.[28] The conflict among aesthetic, referential, and ethical values and their role in representation emerge in Maggie's *Bildungsroman*.

The seriousness of the text's play is consistent with the specular dimension of its use of metaphor and dialogue. Aesthetic play is given moral and cognitive power without being deprived of its freedom, contingency, or reference.

8
Character: Maggie Verver's Ontological Voyage

> *Nous croyons savoir exactement les choses, et ce que pensent les gens, pour la simple raison que nous ne nous en soucions pas. Mais dès que nous avons le désir de savoir, comme a le jaloux, alors c'est un vertigineux kaléidoscope où nous ne distinguons plus rien.*[1]
> —Marcel Proust

IN the famous recognition scene of *The Ambassadors*, Strether discovers that the young couple about whom he has been fantasizing is in fact Chad and Mme de Vionnet and that his assumption about their sexual innocence is mistaken. What is the reader to do with this mistake? Since both the Parisians and those from Woollett are "right" about the relationship, we could categorize Strether's error as an "illusion," as Balzac categorizes the blunders of his heroes. Yet the Jamesian *Bildungsroman* is not simply about correcting empirical errors but exploring the consequences of linguistic and social practices. In *Les Illusions perdues*, the differences between Lucien's illusory provincial readings of Parisian society and the actual forces named by the narrator and the initiated characters are clearly marked and mastered by a realistic discourse that the reader is encouraged to accept. Moreover, the dynamics of Lucien's interior life (thoughts and desires) are socialized and named. In *L'Education sentimentale* the authority of realistic discourse to identify and contain social forces outside the hero and the desires within him is undermined. Language is no longer simply an instrument for adjudicating between truth and illusion but an intimate part of our being. The Jamesian text does not mount such an assault on the practices of realism but points to the irrelevance of its presuppositions. Instead, the Jamesian *Bildungsroman* dramatizes the tensions between and within linguistic practices. Thus, in *The Ambassadors*,

Strether struggles with two speech communities—Woollett and Paris—even though he does not define himself within either one. During the course of the novel, we watch him evolve his own linguistic practice so that his mistake about Chad cannot be reduced to "illusion." In the Jamesian *Bildungsroman*, characters do not "progress" toward a fixed knowledge that is mapped out by the initiators and the narrator. The nature of their problems forces them outside the linguistic practices in which they have lived and into uncharted semantic space.

In Volume II of *The Golden Bowl*, Maggie Verver's *Bildungsroman* begins. At this point, she is wrenched from the Verver system that has defined her and her world and forced into epistemological and ontological uncertainty. My discussion falls into two parts: a synoptic analysis of Maggie in Volume I and a close examination of her predicament in Volume II.

I

The epithet that critics most frequently apply to Maggie in Book I is "innocent" (Yeazell, Norrman, Wilson, and others). Even Fanny, our ficelle, reads the heroine in this way when she proclaims at the end of Volume I that Maggie will be forced to learn " 'what's called Evil—with a very big E: for the first time in her life. To the discovery of it, to the knowledge of it, to the crude experience of it' " (I, 385).[2] I do not wish so much to contest this reading as to put her "innocence" in the context of the Ververs' system and of my foregoing analysis in order to distinguish my reading from the realistic readings of her character.

The crucial feature of Maggie's innocence is not her ignorance—she knows certain sociological information about the characters and a good deal about "the ways of the world"—but the role of innocence in the Verver system. The Ververs divide the world into the undifferentiated sphere that includes father and daughter and the alien sphere outside. The alien sphere is either beautiful—and thus to be appreciated and acquired, or ugly—thus to be ignored. Maggie says to her father, " 'I don't think we lead, as regards other people, any life at all' " (I, 175). The Ververs' insulation from others is ethical and epistemological. The Prince recognizes that "knowledge wasn't one of their needs and that they were in fact constitutionally inaccessible to it" (I, 334). Adam's interest in knowledge is limited to information about works of art and the art market: "He cared that a work of art of price should 'look like' the master to whom it might perhaps be deceitfully attributed; but he had ceased on the whole to know any matter of the rest of life by its looks" (I, 146–47). Art, for Adam, is a sacred domain that redeems the past and makes possible the "passive" goodness of the present; at the same time, art is exchangeable with the other mystified medium, money. When Adam unintentionally leaves the terrain of their discourse by asking his daughter what girls tell each other, Maggie reproaches him, " '[H]ow do I know, father, what vulgar girls do?' " (I, 186).

Even though her marriage brings her into intimate contact with a non-Verver, she still avoids referential discourse: "It was no secret to Maggie—it was indeed positively a public joke for her—that she couldn't explain as Mrs. Assingham did . . ." (I, 160). "She [Fanny] admitted accordingly that she was educative—which Maggie was so aware that she herself inevitably wasn't; so it came round to being true that what she was most in charge of was his mere intelligence. This left, goodness knew, plenty of different calls for Maggie . . ." (I, 161–62). The Ververs' willful insulation from practical discourse—i.e., discourse that purports to refer, explain or convey information, discourse that engages the Kantian faculty of understanding—emerges most clearly in their quest for the beautiful and their reduction of people to fine things. Maggie calls the Prince " 'an object of beauty, an object of price' " (I, 12), while Adam calls him "perfect crystal" (I, 138). Art has tremendous value but no meaning outside of its "fineness." The spectator, the collector feels only a benign pleasure before works of art. Works do not threaten their sense of the world; they only gratify them. The art/acquisition nexus, by which Adam reinscribes rather than transcends his past, is the Ververs' ultimate strategy for dealing with world. Maggie proudly announces Adam's monomania, when she calls the museum, "the work of his life and the motive of everything he does" (I, 12). Even with each other, art is the ground for language. In this passage, Adam generates an analogy for his relationship with Maggie that accommodates and contains the acquisition of the Prince: "At first, certainly, their decent little old-time union, Maggie's and his own, had resembled a good deal some pleasant public square, in the heart of an old city, into which a great Palladian church, say—something with a grand architectural front—had been dropped. . . . By some such process in fine had the Prince, for his father-in-law, while remaining solidly a feature, ceased to be at all ominously a block" (I, 135–36).

The extraordinary assumptions and economic power of the Ververs permit them to wear a mantle of innocence and idealism in their own minds and those of others (except for Charlotte) while crushing all who come in contact with them. The brutality of this innocence emerges in the first chapter when Maggie and the Prince discuss Americans, who, the Prince maintains, are "incredibly romantic." Maggie defines this romanticism as the capacity to make " 'everything so nice' " (I, 11). Amerigo finds the Ververs' romanticism unusual since it seems to offer " 'innocent pleasures, pleasures without penalties.' " He finds out that innocence is not so innocuous.

The Ververs assume (insist) that others who enter their circle—Charlotte, the Prince, the Assinghams—play by the Ververs' rules. Even when Charlotte and the Prince are at the height of their independence, Fanny recognizes that the forms that the quartet follows are " 'those they *impose* on Charlotte and the Prince' " (I, 391). Others' differences are ignored or trivialized by their placement in the "museum" of life.[3] The Ververs' own way is invisible to them. When the Prince remarks on Adam's form, Maggie finds the comment incomprehensible. Adam is not one of several possibilities in the realm of the good. There is no ground for this figure. He is a presence and an assumption. She can only reply: " 'It strikes me he hasn't got any' " (I, 7). When the Prince insists that he has his "way," she calls it "the American way." The Prince, who is outside the Verver system, as his question illustrates, is nonetheless a beautiful object. Maggie invites Amerigo to agree to enter her system, her set of assumptions: " 'Do you think it [the American way] would be good for *you?*' " (I, 7). If the Prince accustoms himself to producing the proper forms, he will become predictable. Predictability of signifiers is what counts for Maggie, not comprehension. The Verver system asks people to produce predictable forms, to become temporally extended objects whose sentences are beautiful and regular. Predictability—which is often taken for knowledge in the sciences—is here one of the ways that Maggie and her father avoid confronting the question of what someone is.

From the beginning of their relationship, Maggie's interest in the Prince is displaced from "him" onto the associations that surround him. Her love for him begins not when she meets him but only when she subsequently learns that one of his names is Amerigo: " 'The Prince was from the start helped with the dear Ververs by *his* wearing it [the name]. The connexion became romantic for Maggie the moment she took it in; she filled out, in a flash, every link that might be vague' " (I, 79). After their marriage the couple discusses the Prince's identity, which he divides into two parts, the public history of his family and his " 'single self, the unknown ... personal quantity' " (I, 9). When he maintains the Ververs know only his public part, Maggie cheerfully confesses that the public, romantic associations, not his personal qualities, are what have interested her:

> "What was it else," Maggie Verver had also said, "that made me originally think of you? It wasn't—as I should suppose you must have seen—what you call your unknown quantity, your particular self. It was the generations behind you, the follies and the crimes, the plunder and the waste. . . . Where, therefore"—she had put it to him again—"without your archives, annals, infamies, would you have been?" (I, 9–10)

Maggie's reduction of the Prince to a work of art or a romantic history parallels her efforts to keep her conversations with the Prince free of practical consequences, to keep them in the realm of "mere play." When Maggie and the Prince discuss their relationships with each other and Adam, the narrator explains the Princess's continuation of the dialogue by "the mere play of her joy" (I, 8). In this dialogue both Maggie and Amerigo indulge in figural play. (The Prince and Adam are likened to crème de volaille and chicken, the Prince to a work of art in the Verver collection, and Maggie's beliefs about Amerigo to water-tight compartments.) However, the Prince arrests this play when he brings in the question of reference. He asks the Princess if she believes that he is not a hypocrite, a deceiver and if that belief is "water-tight." Maggie's momentary astonishment makes him recognize that he has broken one of the Verver codes: "He had perceived on the spot that any *serious* discussion of veracity, of loyalty, or rather of the want of them, practically took her unprepared, as if it were quite new to her. He had noticed it before: It was the English, the American sign that duplicity, like 'love,' had to be joked about. It couldn't be 'gone into' " (I, 15). What underlies metaphoric play for Maggie is that it is superfluous, that it does not threaten the ground of the discussion. When deceit becomes a topic, however, the distinction between real and superfluous language, between what the Prince is and the language used to represent him, is effaced. In an effort that anticipates her struggle in Volume II, Maggie seriously and desperately expands her compartment-analogy in an attempt to contain the Prince's threat: " 'Water-tight—the biggest compartment of all? Why it's the best cabin and the main deck and the engine-room and the steward's pantry! It's the ship itself—it's the whole line' " (I, 15).

Maggie is thus not a confident manipulator; she is immersed in the Verver system and at its mercy. Lacking Adam's feeling of power, she is assailed by anxieties about her relations with the Prince and others. She confesses to her father, " '. . . I do always by nature tremble for my life. That's the way I live' " (I, 181). She even turns her feelings of sexual submission to the Prince into a ground for telling titillating stories in which she is the Prince's victim. Violations are "harmless" in fiction, and these stories take on the function of centering their relationship. In this story, Maggie's desire renders her a passive and helpless victim. Desire cannot be translated into a referential language or action but only into a narrative that justifies her inaction: "If all women feel this way, I should too." Moreover, Maggie inscribes this marital game within the Verver system since we learn of the practice only when Maggie recounts it to her father.

> One of the most comfortable things between the husband and wife meanwhile—one of those easy certitudes they could be merely gay about—was that she never admired him so much . . . as when she saw other women reduced to the same passive pulp that had then begun, once for all, to constitute *her* substance. There was really nothing they had talked of together with more intimate and familiar pleasantry than of the license and privilege, the boundless happy margin, thus established for each: she going so far as to put it that, even should he some day get drunk and beat her, the spectacle of him with hated rivals would . . . suffice to bring her round. (I, 164–65)

The Ververs' system is threatened by Maggie herself when she approaches Adam and suggests that he marry. The static self-satisfaction of their relationship is an active force that she must confront: "Their rightness, the justification of everything—something they so felt the pulse of—sat there with them" (I, 167). The power of this system renders difference powerless: "In their high conditions and with the easy tradition, the almost inspiring allowances, of the house in question, no individual line, however freely marked, was pronounced anything more than funny" (I, 330). The Ververs' disinterest in difference, in knowledge, is represented by a personification of judgment: "Judgement, the spirit with the scales, might perfectly have been imaged there [at the Ververs' home] as some rather snubbed and subdued but quite trained and tactful poor relation . . ." (I, 331). In order to introduce a change, the Princess must point to a lack in the present system. She does so by comparing the present to a more balanced past: " 'What I feel is that there's somehow something that used to be right and that I've made wrong. It used to be right that you hadn't married and that you didn't seem to want to' " (I, 171). Then shifting the ground of her argument, Maggie suggests that they (she and Adam) might be grander than they are (I, 176). Such a possibility dissimulates change under the spatial metaphor of enlargement. To make themselves grander, they can add Charlotte (I, 180–81). Annexation and collection suggest containment by the original group. With the apparently docile Prince on one side of the mantelpiece—Adam is content "that the Prince by good fortune, hadn't proved angular" (I, 136)—Charlotte will restore the symmetry and increase the vibrations of their contentment.

II

When Volume II opens, Maggie has come to sense something, something that has no existence or meaning in the Verver system; hence, it is something that casts Maggie into an epistemological and ontological vertigo and that the narrator represents with the analogy of the pagoda, as we saw in the last chapter. This analogy provides the logical space for figuring her experience and alienation from the system that she thought she knew and the self she thought she was. The Princess tries to signal her recognition by an action that can only be called "something" and in her retrospection she experiences this something, tries to get "nearer to something indeed that she couldn't, that she wouldn't, even to herself, describe" (I, 10), by her return to Portland Place. I have deliberately refused to paraphrase or define "something" with a phrase such as "her recognition of the Prince's complicity with Charlotte." Such a paraphrase reduces her revelation to the comprehension of certain information, as if she were to read about someone else's problem. For Maggie, this revelation is a plunge into uncertainty about the constitution of her social world, a plunge that alters both subject and object.

In the beginning of Book Fourth, we see Maggie struggling to bridge the gap between the disruptive experience and the Verver system. At first, the gap is so extraordinary that the narrator intervenes with his own analogies. When the text moves closer to Maggie's conscious formulations, we read the nonmetaphoric propositions about the past that I cited in the preceding chapter ("She had surrendered herself to her husband without the shadow of reserve . . ." (II, 5]).

In order to understand the present, however, Maggie is forced out of the literal into analogies of her own. She starts by isolating her conversation with the Prince the evening of his return from Matcham and then turns these events into a thing whose meaning is determined: "It had been a poor thing, but it had been all her own, and the whole passage was backwardly there, a great picture hung on the wall of her daily life for her to make what she would of" (II, 10–11). The period is then represented through past perfect narration with extensive use of free indirect discourse (II, 11–12). She tries to contain what she does not know ("accumulations of the unanswered") by turning her ignorance into things, quantities that she can put away: "They were *there*, these accumulations; they were like a roomful of confused objects, never as yet 'sorted,' which for some time now she had been passing and re-passing, along the corridor of her life. She passed it when she could without opening the door; then, on occasion, she turned the key to throw in a fresh contribution" (II, 14). Her figures of containment enable her to proceed without confronting the nature of these things.

Maggie also breaks out in imagined conversations to fill up the stressful space that surrounds and inhabits her. These conversations are attempts to make an explanatory bridge between Maggie's old self with her husband and the discontinuity she feels and wants to articulate:

> " 'Why, why' have I made this evening such a point of our not all dining together? Well, because I've all day been so wanting you alone that I finally couldn't bear it. . . . [T]here comes a day when something snaps, when the full cup, filled to the very brim, begins to flow over. That's what has happened to my need of you." (II, 18)

These voluble explanatory and imaginary conversations contrast with the tense exchanges in the actual conversations, conversations that do not proceed for long according to a common premise about what something is or how it can be explained but that instead force the interlocutors to shift their stances. Thus, Maggie's unspoken discourse is not what she really means or a gloss on what is actually said; rather, it is on the same level as her meditations or her conversations and can be read against realistic discourse in which speech flows from an uncontested ontology. Her imaginary conversations are in this sense "more realistic" than the actual conversations. This imaginary dialogue is followed by a lengthy meditation and Maggie's arrival at a plan, a plan to make the Prince recognize a difference: "She said to herself in her excitement that it was perfectly simple: to bring about a difference, touch by touch, without letting either of the three, and least of all her father, so much as suspect her hand" (II, 33). The word "difference," which recurs frequently in the text, marks a spot in logical space but does not designate any specific action or meaning. "Difference" is defined by opposition to the Verver system, to what was. At the moment, this difference is unthinkable for the Princess; it is an unknown point—and here the spatial metaphor collapses—that she must posit as existing, though she is not sure where. It also becomes an end, a goal toward which she can direct her actions and thoughts.

Thus, many critics' idea of Maggie as "artist" who brings about a change in the two couples is a bit misleading. Maggie sees that she wants to insinuate a difference but she cannot see any farther. Her desire cannot be translated into a statement such as "get her husband back." Moreover, her plan does not succeed in the ordinary sense of the word. There is no teleology that the text follows. (Maggie tries to construct one retrospectively in the last chapter, II, 367.) "What" she achieves at the end is problematic, and she makes the Prince, Charlotte and her father suffer, even if they never wrench a statement from her in which she states "her hand." Thus, Maggie's interior discourse is like Charlotte's dialogue with the Prince that I analyzed in Chapter 6. Maggie must install a difference, establish a referent that is outside her present system of thought, try to make the Prince and Charlotte recognize it and try to understand what this difference means for her and the others. The dialectic between the assertion of a referent and speculation on the nature of that referent is the same for interior discourse as it is for dialogue. The "mind" (conscious or unconscious) is not a privileged space in which authoritarian, true discourse is situated. (*L'Education* also equates interior monologue and public speech.) If realistic discourse relies on the narrator's authority, stream of consciousness (*monologue intérieur*) relies on the unity and authority of interior discourse. *The Golden Bowl* represents the eruption of the unknown within the system of discourse (interior and exterior) and the adaptation by the system to this unknown. Maggie is always trying to work out a new system by making her new actions "consistent": "She was never alone with him [Amerigo], it was to be said, without her having sooner or later to ask herself what had already become of her consistency" (II, 139). "Consistency" here means not only logical coherence but a thickness of her self, a coalescence of her being.

Maggie finds that installing this difference in her relationships with the Prince and Charlotte is complicated by their refusal to take her apparently unusual actions as a difference: "The very liberality of this accommodation might indeed have appeared in the event to give its own account of the matter—as if it had fairly written the Princess down as a person of variations and had accordingly conformed but to a rule of tact in accepting these caprices for law" (II, 36). The personified "liberality" leads to the recognition that Amerigo and Charlotte are together in their response, that "they were *treating* her" (II, 41).

This recognition explodes her plan, her sense of the world, and she is lost again. The narrator intervenes with an analogy ("she might have been picking small shining diamonds out of the sweepings of her ordered house" [II, 42]); and then the solidarity of her present self with the one that sat waiting for Amerigo is broken, and she sees her past in a new way: "[S]he had responsibly shut in, as we have understood, shut in there with her sentient self, only the fact of his reappearance and the plenitude of his presence. These things had been testimony after all to supersede any other, for on the spot, even while she looked, the warmly-washing wave had travelled far up the strand. She had subsequently lived . . . under the dizzying smothering welter . . ." (II, 42–43). This revelation is not immediately integrated into her self but remains distant, becomes another self, a separate observatory: "the prime impression had remained, in the manner of a spying servant, on the other side of the barred threshold" (II, 43). The centrifugal forces of the text raise so many possibilities for Maggie in the next three chapters that the narrator introduces a maxim to motivate the extraordinary currents that pass through the Princess: "We have each our own way of making up for our unselfishness, and Maggie, who had no small self at all as against her husband or her father and only a weak and uncertain one as against her step mother, would verily at this crisis have seen Mrs. Assingham's personal life or liberty sacrificed without a pang" (II, 101).

Nonetheless, Maggie also tries to understand her recognition of things causally, historically, in the manner of a realistic novel. When she asks Fanny " 'what awfulness . . . is between them' " (II, 107), the Princess sees something that reminds her of "what this companion had been expecting":

> She had been watching it come, come from afar, and now it was there.... It was there because of the Sunday luncheon...; it was there, as strangely as one would, because of the bad weather...; it was there because it stood for the whole sum of the perplexities and duplicities among which our young woman felt herself lately to have picked her steps; it was there because Amerigo and Charlotte were again paying together alone a "week-end" visit...; it was there because she had kept Fanny, on her side, from paying one. (II, 108)

Maggie so overburdens causality with empirical (bad weather) and symbolic ("it stood for") sentences that causality functions as a demonstrative, as a means of locating "it" rather than explaining "it". The explanations find/create the object. Thus, Maggie's plea to Fanny (" 'Help me find out what I imagine' ") is not simply evidence of the Princess's naïveté or her lack of information; it is a plea to help her stabilize her speculations.

If my reading of the text seems to emphasize its instability and ambiguity, the Assinghams provide us with another "text" in Book Fourth, chapter 7. Fanny is concerned that the Ververs may discover the facts about her past involvement with the Prince and Charlotte and that the Ververs may give some perfectly plausible but condemning explanations for her behavior: " 'It would have been seen, it would have been heard of before, the case of the woman a man doesn't want, or of whom he's tired.... *Cela s'est vu*, my dear' " (II, 127–28). However, Fanny then rejects these realistic readings of her actions since Maggie will not use them. In defining her own rule for the Princess, Fanny also defines Maggie's plan with a precision that escapes Maggie herself: " 'Well, this summer at Fawns to begin with. She can live as yet of course but from hand to mouth; but she has worked it out for herself, I think, that the very danger of Fawns, superficially looked at, may practically amount to a greater protection" (II, 132). The Assinghams thus write realistic narrative of socialized desire that the rest of the text refuses. However, the Assinghams do not take their version of the relationships among the characters for truth, nor do they dismiss it as a "mere" story. Their conversation is an iterative dialogue, and the narrator insists on this aspect throughout with phrases such as "on each occasion" (II, 126), "each time" (II, 127). The Colonel takes pleasure in the predictability of the story they tell: "He was well enough aware by this time of what she finally did think, but he wasn't without a sense again also for his amusement by the way. It would have made him, for a spectator of these passages between the pair, resemble not a little the artless child who hears his favourite story told for the twentieth time and enjoys it exactly because he knows what is next to happen" (II, 128). This ritualistic repetition of a realistic story becomes a means to stabilize their imaginations and control their anxieties.

The Princess's discovery of the bowl at the end of Book Fourth changes the forces that the Assinghams try to narrate. It confirms the hypothesis that she has been acting under since the beginning of Volume II. Her discovery of the facts gets its value not so much from the revelatory knowledge that it gives but from its demonstrability in the eyes of the Prince. The bowl gives Maggie power not only to manipulate her husband but the power to change his conception of her. The bowl is a difference that he will have to recognize, a difference that will not just be a tool to bind him but that will alter what they are. The discovery of the bowl is thus an ending—its placement at the end of Book Fourth—as well as the beginning of a new sense of being and a new referential language for Maggie.

The narratological features of the novel support this reading. Her discovery is not reported directly or retrospectively by the narrator. We get no inside view of Maggie's reactions or meditations at that time. Instead, the text concentrates on the effect of the discovery on her relationship with Amerigo. Maggie herself tells the story, and it is a simple report of events designed only to get the Prince to agree to the proposition that she knows; she does not want to crush him. Our inside view of Maggie some time after her return from the shop shows not outraged innocence but the vision of the new possibility "that her husband would have on the whole question a new need of her, a need which was in fact being born between them in these very seconds. It struck her truly as so new that he would have felt hitherto none to compare with it at all; would indeed absolutely by this circumstance be *really* needing her for the first time in their whole connexion" (II, 186). The recognition of this need is followed by the recognition of a new identity for herself, of the possibility of becoming someone mysterious and attractive to the Prince: " 'Yes, look, look,' she seemed to see him hear her say even while her sounded words were other—'look, look, both at the truth that still survives in that smashed evidence and at the even more remarkable appearance that I'm not such a fool as you supposed me. Look at the possibility that since I *am* different there may still be something in it for you' " (II, 187–88).

The Prince resists assenting to the statement that there is a difference. After Maggie begins her story (II, 188), the Prince tells his version in which the events point to nothing, in which the events have no consequences for their past system of living. (" 'I don't see, you must let me say, the importance or the connexion' " [II, 195]). When the Princess continues to build her case on the shopkeeper, the Prince tries to escape by attacking the shopkeeper. Maggie only shakes her head "as if, no, after consideration, not *that* way were an issue" (II, 197). Maggie does not want an explanation; she wants him to hear her statements without denying them. These statements are not only about the bowl but about herself: " 'My only point now, at any rate,' she went on, 'is the difference, as I say, that it may make for *you*. Your knowing was—from the moment you did come—in all I had in view. . . . Your knowing that I've ceased . . . to be as I was. *Not* to know' " (II, 201–2).

Maggie identifies knowing and being here.[4] She wants him to see that she is different; she does not simply want him back in the fold in the way it was. Her final challenge (" 'Find out for yourself' ") is not just about what Adam knows but what she is. If we were to follow the language of means and ends, of teleology, in the text, we could say that Maggie's goal in Book Fourth is to get the Prince to recognize her difference, that her goal in Book Fifth is to deny this difference to Adam and Charlotte (though not in the same way), and that her goal in Book Sixth is to bless and affirm this difference. I want to distinguish this language from the language of knowledge and being. If Maggie is certain that the Prince has "taken in" her difference, she is not certain about what this means for herself and others. Thus, her pact with the Prince is a *point de repère* outside her system of meaning. In Book Fifth Maggie feels her way to consistency, to closing and containing by getting her father and Charlotte to agree to certain statements. In all three parts of Volume II she has moments when the terrifying unknown that surrounds this reference point invades her, when she sees that the teleological tightrope that she creates and walks is strung over an abyss into which she casts metaphors in order to keep her balance.

Maggie emerges from the passage with the Prince feeling that she has been raised above murky suppositions, and her success is represented with optical analogies: "the change brought about by itself as great a difference of view as the shift of an inch in the position of a telescope. It was her telescope in fact that gained in range . . ." (II, 207). Maggie's sense of mastery even reaches the point where the narrator invokes the analogy of authorship to represent her feelings of control over the others: "they might have been figures rehearsing some play of which she herself was the author" (II, 235). She is like the author of the Jamesian tales, for she holds the secret for which the characters search: "the key to the mystery, the key that could wind and unwind it without a snap of the spring, was there in her pocket" (II, 236). "Authorship" and physical possession are part of the semantic fields of containment, which Maggie uses to fix and divide her world. Containment is not the equivalent of knowledge, however. Like the secrets in the tales, Maggie's secret—in this case her conversation with the shopkeeper—cannot be reduced to the informational content of the secret. Rather, this opacity pervades all that Maggie says and does and it consequently changes all the characters.

The narrator also checks Maggie's sense of mastery, her authorship by bringing her attempt to write her story up against fragments that resist her constructions and that call up radically different alternatives: "it was a scene she might people, by the press of her spring, either with serenities and dignities and decencies, or with terrors and shames and ruins, things as ugly as those formless fragments of her golden bowl she was trying so hard to pick up" (II, 236).

The narrator takes up the deconstructive potential of the bowl, the story that Maggie cannot author but that she vaguely senses: "[I]f the beauty of appearances had been so consistently preserved, it was only the golden bowl as Maggie herself knew it that had been broken. The breakage stood not for any wrought discomposure among the triumphant three—it stood merely for the dire deformity of her attitude toward them. She was unable at the minute, of course, fully to measure the difference thus involved for her . . ." (II, 240). When Charlotte leaves the card game and approaches the Princess, Maggie looks back on the players, the characters in her play, without a sense of closure. She has a sense of power but not of knowledge: "Side by side for three minutes they fixed this picture of quiet harmonies, the positive charm of it and, as might have been said, the full significance—which, as was now brought home to Maggie, could be no more after all than a matter of interpretation, differing always for a different interpreter" (II, 243–44). Maggie is able to escape from her encounter with the unknown by her adherence to her "plan," by her resolve to treat the others as means to an end. Thus, in her conversation with the Prince in the penultimate chapter when the pressure of the bracketed world of desire threatens to emerge too soon, Maggie and the Prince adhere to the plan and enjoin each other with the same request, "wait": "It was the word of his own distress and entreaty, the word for both of them, all they had left, their plank now on the great sea" (II, 352–53).

Maggie's alienation from the Verver system does not mean that she abandons her former principles. Rather, she attempts to make changes that are consistent with the system and that involve her in a whirlwind of identity and difference. This problem comes out most clearly in her conversations with her father. In their first conversations in Volume II (Book Fourth before the discovery of the bowl), Maggie is sensitive to Adam's perception of a change, and she reads his looks: " 'Everything's remarkably pleasant, isn't it?—but *where* for it after all are we? up in a balloon and whirling through space or down in the depths of the earth . . .'" (II, 73). The unspoken difference between past and present haunts Maggie—the past hangs "behind them like a framed picture in a museum" (II, 85)—but she takes Adam's lead, his decision "to *imitate* . . . the ancient tone of gold" (II, 86). The tension between similarity (continuity) and difference (discontinuity) is resolved in an agreement to dissimulate difference and to let Maggie run the show: "His recognition of the new terms as different from the old, what was that practically but a confession that something had happened . . ." (II, 98).

In Book Fifth, Maggie's dialogue reveals not only her commitment to her plan and her attachment to her father but her discovery of passion. For Maggie, this excursion with her father is not a repetition of their most recent conversation but of the conversation they had years before in which Maggie suggested to Adam that he marry. If the present can imitate the prelapsarian dialogue, then the Verver system can be preserved and difference denied: "Well then that other sweet evening was what the present sweet evening would resemble" (II, 255). Maggie is not tortured by the consequences of the present for the Ververs as she was in the preceding scene. She is so swept up in the sense of power that she no longer tries to efface the differences between past and present but to fuse them so that her passions move freely between her husband and her father:

> It was positively as if in short the inward felicity of their being once more, perhaps only for half an hour, simply daughter and father had glimmered out for them. . . . They were husband and wife—oh so immensely!—as regards other persons [the syntactic structure reinforces the sexual connotations since the qualifying phrase appears as an after-thought]. . . . [I]t was wonderfully like their having got together into some boat and

> paddled off from the shore where husbands and wives, luxuriant complications, made the air too tropical.... Why... couldn't they always live, so far as they lived together, in a boat? (II, 254–55)

Maggie wants to isolate her father and their common system from the change that she wants to initiate. She begins by asking him to separate from the others for a private talk. Physical and conceptual isolation go together in this text. Almost all of the dialogues are between two people between whom a unique and unpredictable linguistic medium emerges. Apart from the others, the Ververs exist in their medium, deal with forces in a different way than Maggie does when she speaks to someone else. However, once the conversation begins, Maggie's discourse forces Adam to recognize a discontinuity with the past. Maggie's reassertion of the identity of the past and the present betrays a difference within the identity by her aggressiveness, her self-consciousness and her intensity. Maggie's speech on love is Adam's first shock:

> "My idea is this, that when you only love a little you're naturally not jealous—or are only jealous also a little, so that it doesn't matter. But when you love in a deeper and intenser way, then you're in the very same proportion jealous; your jealousy has intensity and, no doubt, ferocity. When however you love in the most abysmal and unutterable way of all—why then you're beyond everything, and nothing can pull you down." (II, 262)

The force of this desire puts her "beyond everything" and at a loss to know where she is (II, 263).

Her confession of the way she loves the Prince (and Adam) puts her outside the Verver system. Her metamorphosis into a character full of sexuality and her attempt to articulate this region of desire threaten Adam's aestheticism, which reduces desire to the regulated hum of satisfaction, which reduces relationships to fine art and time to the intervals between new acquisitions. Adam absorbs the effect of her speech: "He sat a while as if he knew himself hushed, almost admonished, and not for the first time" (II, 263). Adam repeats part of Maggie's declaration (" 'I guess I've never been jealous' " [II, 264]), in hopes of understanding and binding with her again. (Repetition in James is frequently a plea for understanding and solidarity, as we saw with Fanny and the Colonel and the Prince and Charlotte.)

However, Maggie keeps Adam off balance by picking another part of her statement for emphasis—"Oh it's you, father, who are what I call beyond everything" (II, 264)—and attributing it to him.

Maggie then shifts the conversation to an assertion that she is selfish and that Adam is her victim. In response to Adam's protest, Maggie claims that her accusation is correct even though she did not ask Adam to go back to American City after her marriage (II, 270–71). Adam, of course, reads this irrelevant qualification as a suggestion that he become her victim and leave: " 'You regularly make me wish that I *had* shipped back to American City' " (II, 271). Maggie rationalizes the brutality of her own suggestion by attributing the idea to him: "*There* was his idea, the clearness of which for an instant almost dazzled her" (II, 271). The Ververs terminate this pact with statements of faith in each other, and Maggie swells before his greatness: "she was lifted aloft by the consciousness that he was simply a great and deep and high little man ..." (II, 274). She ascribes this value to him through the art analogy: "... her impression rose and rose, even as that of the typical charmed gazer, in the still museum, before the named and dated object, the pride of the catalogue ..." (II, 273–74). Maggie breaks the Verver system and yet closes off the disruption of her break by reasserting the values of her past and her father's authority.

Maggie's escape from her father also produces another uncharacteristic emotion, empathy. Once she sees that Charlotte is contained, that the Prince keeps her in ignorance and that Adam leads her by a "silken halter" (II, 287), Maggie tries to imagine her adversary's experience. The Verver moral system that reduces otherness to the uninteresting and the artifact is supplemented by a sensibility for analogous experience. Having come to feel alienation from the beliefs she thought were shared and accurate, Maggie sees Charlotte as another betrayed woman in pain. With the Princess's empathy, however, is also a voyeuristic curiosity, as if sharing pain will also give her access to Charlotte's knowledge of passion. Maggie suddenly feels herself plunged into this domain of desire, a desire that she controls only by her "plan" but that she does not know and that she cannot imagine. Maggie approaches the glass container into which she has maneuvered Charlotte: "Behind the glass lurked the *whole* history of the relation she had so fairly flattened her nose against it to penetrate—the glass Mrs. Verver might at this stage have been frantically tapping from within by way of supreme irrepressible entreaty" (II, 329).[5] When Maggie imagines what Charlotte could say to her, the Princess articulates what her own future could be like:

"You don't know what it is to have been loved and broken with. You haven't been broken with. You haven't been broken with, because in *your* relation what can there have been worth speaking of to break? Ours was everything a relation could be, filled to the brim with the wine of consciousness; and if it was to have no meaning, no better meaning than that such a creature as you could breathe upon it, at your hour, for blight, why was I myself dealt with all for deception? why condemned after a couple of short years to find the golden flame—oh, the golden flame!—a mere handful of black ashes?" (II, 329–30)

This imagined accusation by Charlotte is as close as Maggie gets to admitting any responsibility for her husband's relationship with Charlotte. The Princess always eulogizes this perfect past to herself and to Adam. The Ververs never make mistakes or changes; they simply move to higher forms of perfection. In Book Sixth, with her separation from Adam imminent, the Princess self-righteously maintains the superiority of her love for her father to that of the lovers: " '... lost to each other really much more than Amerigo and Charlotte are; since for them it's just, it's right, it's deserved, while for us it's only sad and strange and not caused by our fault' " (II, 333).

In the last scene of the novel, Maggie tries to reassert the Verver system and bless the present situation as a fulfillment of their vision. This process begins when Maggie and Adam turn from a painting (which Adam declares is "all right") to the rest of the objects in the room and to Amerigo and Charlotte. "The two noble persons seated in conversation and at tea fell thus into the splendid effect and the general harmony: Mrs. Verver and the Prince fairly 'placed' themselves, however unwittingly, as high expressions of the kind of human furniture required aesthetically by such a scene. The fusion of their presence with the decorative elements, their contribution to the triumph of selection, was complete and admirable" (II, 360). The narrator abruptly undermines this Ververian process of aesthetic acquisition: "though to a lingering view, a view more penetrating than the occasion really demanded, they also might have figured as concrete attestations of a rare power of purchase" (II, 360). This moment of aesthetic contemplation is achieved by bracketing menacing questions of meaning but not of teleology.[6] For Maggie, everyone acts as if he were conspiring to bring her plan to a close, to continue to play out a part that is founded on an unexamined, unknown premise that has emerged to unite them. Maggie sees "the note of that strange accepted finality of relation, as from couple to couple, which almost escaped an awkwardness only by not attempting a gloss.... To do such an hour justice would have been in some degree to question its grounds—which was why they remained in fine, the four of them, in the upper air, united in the firmest abstention from pressure" (II, 361).

When Maggie speaks of Charlotte's impending absence (instead of his) she "saw him the next instant take it—take it in a way that helped her smile to pass all for an allusion to what she didn't and couldn't say" (II, 363). However, what appears to be an evasion of their feelings comes to ground their success after father and daughter agree on Charlotte's greatness: "It was all she might have wished, for it was, with a kind of speaking competence, the note of possession and control; and yet it conveyed to her as nothing till now had done the reality of their parting. They were parting, in the light of it, absolutely on Charlotte's *value*—the value that was filling the room out of which they had stepped as if to give it play..." (II, 365). Maggie closes the conversation with the assertion that their present situation is a fulfillment of the Verver vision: " 'It's success, father' " (II, 366).

After the departure, Maggie has an experience that reinforces her affirmation, an experience that opens a retrospective vista that justifies and terminates the process begun the night of the Prince's return from Matcham:

> [B]ut everything now, as she vaguely moved about, struck her as meaning so much that the unheard chorus swelled. Yet *this* above all—her just being there as she was and waiting for him to come in, their freedom to be together there always—was the meaning most disengaged.... She knew at last really why—and how she had been inspired and guided, how she had been persistently able, how to her soul all the while it had been for the sake of this end. Here it was then, the moment, the golden fruit that had shone from afar. (II, 367)

The Princess strings a teleology through her past, an intention (identity) that links Maggie at the beginning of Volume II to Maggie at the end. My analysis in the foregoing chapters shows the impossibility of such a synthesis. Maggie is not a continuous but discontinuous being. "What" she intended at the beginning of Volume II could hardly be realized since the situation is inconceivable to her at the beginning of the volume. Moreover, her epiphany is only teleological and not ontological, a confusion that she frequently makes but that the text refuses. Throughout Volume II Maggie suspends questions about being and knowledge in order to realize (improvise) a plan the vague purpose of which is to introduce a difference that will separate the Prince and Charlotte and that will make her interesting to her husband. The consequences of this difference for her own identity or those of the others are terrifying abysses into which she must avoid looking. The unifying teleological reading of her life is reopened in the next sentence following her revelation, when she moves from thinking in terms of means and ends to problems of being and knowledge: "only what *were* these things in the fact, for the hand and for the lips, when tested, when tasted—what were they as a reward?" (II, 367). She tries to control these questions by carrying out the metaphoric potential of "golden fruit" and "reward" through a grid of exchange, a Verver favorite: "Closer than she had ever been to the measure of her course and the full face of her act, she had an instant of the terror that, when there has been suspense, always precedes, on the part of the creature to be paid, the certification of the amount. Amerigo knew it, the amount" (II, 367). Maggie tries to keep the Prince on the subject of their plan by posing a question about Charlotte. However, Amerigo is playing no longer. Maggie does not find her reward but the pressure of the man she has sequestered but scarcely known, the man whose intense concentration on her alone casts her into the unknown again: " 'See'? I see nothing but *you*.' And the truth of it had with this force after a moment so strangely lighted his eyes that as for pity and dread of them she buried her own in his breast" (II, 369).

The golden fruit embodies two different teleologies. The one she constructs with Adam has its origin in Volume I and makes the present a fulfillment of the plan that has not changed the planners. When she thinks about the past with regard to the Prince, however, the story of the fruit begins in Volume II with the difference that she introduces. The fruit must contain both identity and difference, and this tension erupts when Maggie confronts the Prince. Nor does the text propose a teleological closure for the reader. The fluctuations in the text's ontology block in any attempt to draw linear development. This path is parodied for the reader by the protagonist's two conflicting attempts at recuperation, much in the way Frédéric's two novelistic versions of his life confront the jagged fragments of the text the reader has just finished. The Jamesian ending does not complete a formalistic wholeness but recircuits the forces of signification. In Amerigo's last statement, "nothing" annihilates the text to this point. The indexicals "I" and "you" are thus cut loose from their previous meanings. Their reference points toward a space of desire where the reader joins the characters in the task of rereading.

Conclusion

THUS, *Les Illusions perdues, L'Education sentimentale,* and *The Golden Bowl* are not simply three realistic novels with different themes and techniques. Such a reading locates the texts in the narrow grid of empiricism and psychologism in which subject and object are entities that await the passive labels of language. This study reverses the priority so that language calls the world into being. Reference is language's power of disclosure, which is not a simple matter of designation but a force that emerges through linguistic practices. "Realism" is thus not the measure of representational "accuracy" but a particular set of practices. Each of the eight chapters isolates a particular novelistic problem and shows how the texts of Balzac, Flaubert, and James work out different referential strategies that make different demands on the reader.

In *Les Illusions perdues,* the narrator's language frames an ultimate semantic system that defines the physical and cultural space of the characters. The characters' own speech and thoughts do not challenge this system but work within it. *L'Education sentimentale* fragments this ontological security. The language of the narrator and the characters creates referential forces that are not in a realistic system, and the characters do not decipher society or communicate. The language of means and ends and the exchange of information that make up a large portion of the traditional realistic novel are trivialized and devalued. Instead of representing a plot in a secure world, *L'Education* dramatizes the tensions of being. The exterior world (perception, speech) and the interior world (reflection, memory) crush the protagonist into silence or they solicit a reverie or a cliché. Subjectivity becomes a space of linguistic currents that wait to be triggered by an experience of value. Frédéric's passage through the novel is a sequence of jolts into separate ontological compartments, a passage in which he learns nothing, in which there is no *Bildung*. Frédéric is caught in a paradoxical dilemma in which he is condemned to repeat himself but never coincide with himself. The world is not fixed and encoded, waiting to be understood by the hero as it is in *Les Illusions perdues*.

The Golden Bowl takes up the dramatization of reference as its central problem. Even though the values of the text and the power it accords consciousness and language are different from those in *L'Education*, both novels are concerned with representing ontological discontinuity of experience and with the role of language in generating and resisting these discontinuities. The known (the semantic system that *Les Illusions perdues* uses as a building block and that *L'Education* cuts loose from reference and signification and ossifies into matter) here appears only as the unspeakably obvious and unimportant that does not locate the objects or the meanings of the world in which the drama is played. In *The Golden Bowl* the characters are forced to confront the limits of their linguistic practices, and they alter these practices by changing the signification of words or gesturing toward new referents. In the beginning of the novel, Maggie and her father define themselves and the world by their system, and they refuse to alter it to accommodate others. All who enter their circle must speak Ververese. Maggie's discovery that "something" is wrong destroys this system, and she falls through an ontological void, where her self and those of others are plunged into the unknown. Unlike Lucien de Rubempré, "what" she learns in the course of the novel is not a socially accessible knowledge. Referents and meanings hurtle past her, burst in on her. She is like Frédéric Moreau in that she is deprived of a masterable semantic system for defining herself and the world. Unlike Frédéric, however, Maggie is aware of her discontinuity, and she tries to discover a language that will contain her experience. If *L'Education* dessicates knowledge into a fragmented impossibility, *The Golden Bowl* multiplies the possibilities for knowledge; however, "knowledge" is different in each of the ontological moments created by the shifting referential languages of the text.

This analysis of Balzac, Flaubert, and James provides a model for discussing the representational strategies not only of nineteenth century novelists such as Dickens, George Eliot and Zola, but also of authors like Sterne and Diderot who wrote before the peculiar paranoia of realistic discourse became such an important concern. Writers such as Proust and Woolf, who, like James, foreground proper names and metaphoric representation at the expense of common nouns and literal designation are obvious candidates. However, the importance of the study of reference is not limited to a narrow corpus of texts; reference brings language, text, and world into a new dialogue. The text is not a self-contained structure or a collection of signifiers and signifieds but a way of disclosing the world. The way a text reinscribes the texts of our world, the way it reroutes reference, becomes a concern not only for linguistics, rhetoric, and philosophy but also ideology. If language constitutes subject and object, then the values embedded in language are not added to referents but coextensive with them. The text thus invites the reader to rediscover the ontological power of language that is not limited to literature. In *An Introduction to Metaphysics* Martin Heidegger says, "Words and language are not wrappings in which things are packed for the commerce of those who write and speak. It is in words and language that things first come into being and are" (11). In the reading of these novels, the reader is offered new languages of being for rewriting the text in which she finds herself written.

Notes

INTRODUCTION

1. "The New Novel," *Literary Criticism: Essays on Literature, American Writers, English Writers* (New York: Library of America, 1984), 159.
2. *Positions*, trans. Alan Bass (Chicago: University of Chicago Press, 1981), 28.
3. *Philosophy and the Mirror of Nature* (Princeton: Princeton University Press, 1979), 371–72.
4. Barthes, *S/Z* (Paris: Seuil, 1970); *Flaubert: The Uses of Uncertainty* (London: Elek Books, 1974); *The Theoretical Dimensions of Henry James* (Madison: University of Wisconsin Press, 1984).
5. See Gerald Graff, *Literature Against Itself: Literary Ideas in Modern Society* (Chicago: University of Chicago Press, 1979). For a trenchant and lucid critique of the attack on deconstruction, see Gregory S. Jay's review of *The Skeptic Disposition in Contemporary Culture*, by Eugene Goodheart, *Genre* 18 (1986): 297–303.
6. *The Consequences of Pragmatism* (Minneapolis: University of Minnesota Press, 1982), 153.
7. See *Positions*, particularly 89–92, where Derrida calls not for a rejection of reference but for reexamination of what has been taken to be the "outside language."
8. *The Resistance to Theory* (Minneapolis: University of Minnesota Press, 1986), 11.
9. "Sense and Reference," in *Translations from the Philosophical Writings of Gottlob Frege*, trans. P. T. Geach and Max Black (Oxford: Blackwell, 1970). The complexities of Frege's theory have been hotly debated. See

Michael Dummett, *Frege: Philosophy of Language* (London: Duckworth, 1973).

10. See Rorty's critique of the tradition of analytic philosophy in *Philosophy and the Mirror of Nature*, 131–311, and Derrida's reading of Husserl in *La voix et le phénomène*.

11. "Le sens et la forme," in *Problèmes de linguistique générale*, II (Paris: Gallimard, 1974).

12. In *On Deconstruction*, Jonathan Culler discusses the inevitability of this opposition, of what he calls the paradox of structure and event: "The structure of a language, its system of norms and regularities, is a product of events, the result of prior speech acts. However, when we take this argument seriously and begin to look at the events which are said to determine structures, we find that every event is itself already determined and made possible by prior structures" (95).

13. For a carefully argued and complex discussion of how "subject" and "world" can be restored within a nonfoundationalist horizon, see Calvin Schrag's *Communicative Praxis and the Space of Subjectivity* (Bloomington: Indiana University Press, 1986). In this view, "the being of the subject is an implicate of communicative praxis—not a foundation for it" (142).

14. *The Rule of Metaphor: Multi-Disciplinary Studies in the Creation of Meaning in Language*, trans. Robert Czerny, with Kathleen McLaughlin and John Costello (Toronto: University of Toronto Press, 1977), 298.

15. See Heidegger's discussion of assertion in *Being and Time*, trans. John Macquarrie and Edward Robinson (New York: Harper, 1962), 195–203, where he maintains that assertion "cannot disown its ontological origin from an interpretation which understands" and distinguishes the "existential-hermeneutic 'as' " and the "apophantical 'as' " of assertion" (201). In his later work, he moves beyond the discussion of language as a structure of *Dasein* and makes it the "House of Being."

16. "Texte, référence, déictique," *Texte* 1 (1982), 122. Morot-Sir, like Ricoeur, synthesizes the contributions of the Anglo-American philosophical tradition with those of Continental philosophy and linguistics. For other studies of reference, see Charles Altieri, *Act and Quality: A Theory of Meaning and Humanistic Understanding* (Amherst: University of Massachusetts Press, 1981), and Umberto Eco, *Semiotics and the Philosophy of Language* (Bloomington: Indiana University Press, 1984). For a readable survey of the analytic school's study of language, see Ian Hacking, *Why Does Language Matter to Philosophy?* (Cambridge: Cambridge University Press, 1975), in which Hacking answers his own question: "It [language] matters for the reason that ideas mattered in seventeenth century philosophy, because ideas then, and sentences now, serve as the interface between the knowing subject and what is known. The sentence matters even more if we begin to dispense with the fiction of the knowing subject, and regard discourse as autonomous" (184).

17. *The Ways of World Making* (Indianapolis: Hackett, 1978). Donald Davidson's well-known essay "On the Very Idea of a Conceptual Scheme," *The Proceedings of the American Philosophical Association* 47 (1973–74): 5–20, argues that we need to abandon the view that poses a variety of schemes versus an uninterpreted reality. (Rorty pursues this in "The World Well Lost" in *Consequences*.) Davidson is right to insist that we must know

or assume a great deal about another's beliefs even to disagree with him or her. The point for my argument is that the supposedly innocuous differences that Davidson is willing to admit—such as disagreement between Fanny and the Colonel in *The Golden Bowl*—can open radical differences between and within characters, differences that are not contained by their shared beliefs.

18. Heidegger, *Early Greek Thinking*, trans. David Farrell Krell and Frank Capuzzi (New York: Harper and Row, 1975), 52.

19. For Balzac and Flaubert, I shall refer first to the page number of the French edition and then to the English translation, which I modify occasionally. I shall use the following editions: *Les Illusions perdues* (Paris: Garnier-Flammarion, 1966); *L'Education sentimentale: Histoire d'un jeune homme* (Paris: Garnier Frères, 1964); *Lost Illusions*, trans. Herbert J. Hunt (New York: Penguin, 1971); *The Sentimental Education*, trans. Robert Baldick (New York: Penguin, 1964); *The Golden Bowl* (New York: Scribners, 1909). Italics indicate the author's emphasis, while underlining indicates my emphasis.

20. See François Jost, "La Tradition du *Bildungsroman*," *Comparative Literature* 21 (1969): 97–115.

21. Auerbach says, "The serious treatment of everyday reality, the rise of more extensive and socially inferior groups to the position of subject matter for problematic-existential representation, on the one hand; on the other, the embedding of random persons and events in the general course of contemporary history, . . . these, we believe are the foundations of modern realism" (*Mimesis: The Representation of Reality in Western Literature*, trans. Willard Trask (Garden City: Doubleday, 1957), 433–34.

22. *Encyclopedia of Philosophy*, ed. Paul Edwards (New York: Macmillan, 1967), VII, 77.

23. *On Realism* (Boston: Routledge and Kegan Paul, 1973), 32.

24. *The Realistic Imagination* (Chicago: University of Chicago Press, 1981), 8.

25. See, for example, Phillip Grover's *Henry James and the French Novel* (London: Elek, 1973). The study of the development of James's novels has also been limited by this psychological realism, which reduces the dynamics of language to James's shift from representation of the external world (in such works as *The American*) to the representation of consciousness in the Major Phase. Ruth Yeazell's *Language and Knowledge in the Late Novels of Henry James* challenges this assumption.

26. James E. Miller says, "To look at reality through the frame of one's consciousness is to frame reality with an individual (unique) point of view—the ultimate source of interest in fiction" ("Henry James in Reality," *Critical Inquiry* 2 [1976]: 595).

27. "Un Discours contraint," *Poétique* 16 (1973); 422.

28. Balzac's novel—like any text—can be deconstructed or read for the play of its codes, as Barthes's reading of "Sarrasine" in *S/Z* illustrates. See also Samuel Weber, *Unwrapping Balzac: A Reading of La Peau de Chagrin* (Toronto: University of Toronto Press, 1979).

29. I discuss these theories more fully in later chapters and show the extraordinary differences between Balzac and James, differences that the loose rubric "realism" or the thematic category of "melodrama" blurs. The

only book devoted entirely to Flaubert and James is David Gervais's *Flaubert and Henry James: A Study in Contrasts* (London: Macmillan, 1978), which is an unusual book with a misleading title. The study focuses on James's, Flaubert's, and Gervais's meaning of the tragic, and the author uses *Madame Bovary* and *The Portrait of a Lady* as contrasting examples. "This study in contrasts, then, has as its final purpose to begin a discussion of the possibility of tragic art in the novels of the nineteenth century" (xii). It is an interesting book but has little to do with my study.

30. This tradition began with Percy Lubbock's *The Craft of Fiction* (1921) and has continued until the present. See R. B. J. Wilson's *Henry James's Ultimate Narrative: The Golden Bowl* (St. Lucia: Queensland Press, 1981). This reading of James's criticism is now being challenged. See David Carroll's *The Subject in Question* (Chicago: University of Chicago Press, 1982) and Rowe's *The Theoretical Dimensions of Henry James*, especially 219–52. My analysis works from the philosophy of language—which Rowe does not treat—to offer a new approach to James's criticism through the dynamics of his fiction. That is, the novels will become a way of reading his prefaces, not vice versa.

31. *Henry James: Literary Criticism (French Writers, Other European Writers, The Prefaces to the New York Edition)* (New York: Library of America, 1984), 150, 312, 326.

CHAPTER 1

1. For details on the operation of disengagement, see A. J. Greimas and J. Courtes, *Semiotics and Language*, trans. Larry Crist et al. (Bloomington: Indiana University Press, 1979), 87–91. This may appear to be simply a fancy way of describing the famous "objectivity" of the text; however, I will show how the label "objectivity" effaces many important features of the text.

2. Cited in René Dumesnil, *L'Education sentimentale de Gustave Flaubert* (Paris: Nizet, 1963), 182.

3. See Brombert's *The Novels of Flaubert: A Study of Themes and Techniques* (Princeton: Princeton University Press, 1966) and Sherrington's *Three Novels by Flaubert: A Study of Techniques* (New York: Oxford University Press, 1970). This division of Flaubert criticism into two camps is an obvious simplification of the diverse readings of *L'Education*, but it provides a useful point of departure for my dialogues with critics. The most comprehensive study in the structuralist tradition is Doris Kadish's "Two Semiological Features of Four Functions of Descriptions: The Example of Flaubert," *Romanic Review* 69 (1979): 278–98. She divides description into four functions: expository, symbolic, structural, and poetic; however, her model effaces the role of the reader, limits historical differences among texts to functions and omits the "effet de réel" that is crucial to *L'Education*. The separation of the poetic from the referential function, widely accepted in semiotics, gets its most influential formulation in Roman Jakobson's model: "this function [the poetic] by promoting the palpability of signs, deepens the fundamental dichotomy of signs and objects" (cited in Kadish, 293). I do not deny the conventional, rhetorical nature of description; however, I see no reason why poetic and referential forces cannot coincide.

4. Balzac's historical asides are well known. See, for example, the discussion of paper (129; 108ff.).

5. *Communications* 11 (1968): 84–89.

6. See Christopher Prendergast's chapter "The Economy of Mimesis," *The Order of Mimesis* (Cambridge: Cambridge University Press, 1986), where he attacks Barthes for reducing "the real" to "referential illusion" and ignoring important problems in the philosophy of language—e.g., the cavalier way that the signified is removed so that we have only a relation between signifier and referent. Although I agree with this critique of Barthes's discussion of reference in this essay, Barthes's piece brings to the surface the idea of "the real" as a thematic category.

7. In *Writer and Critic and Other Essays*, trans. Arthur D. Kahn (New York: Grosset and Dunlap, 1970).

8. See *Flaubert and Postmodernism*, ed. Naomi Schor and Henry F. Majewski (Lincoln: University of Nebraska Press, 1986). Jean-François Lyotard says, "modern aesthetics is an aesthetic of the sublime, though a nostalgic one. It allows the unpresentable to be put forward only as the missing contents; but the form, because of its recognizable consistency, continues to offer the reader pleasure." "The postmodern would be that which ... puts forward the unpresentable in the presentation itself; that which denies itself the solace of good forms, the consensus of a taste which would make it possible to share collectively the nostalgia for the unattainable" ("Answering the Question: What Is Postmodernism?" trans. Régis Durand, in *The Postmodern Condition*, trans. Geoff Bennington and Brian Massumi [Minneapolis: University of Minnesota Press, 1984], 81).

9. *Essais critiques* (Paris: Seuil, 1964), 232.

10. The relationship between the character and the exterior world is frequently discussed by critics. For example, Jean-Pierre Duquette and Robert Sherrington maintain that these descriptions represent "psychological features" of the character or the interaction between subject and object. Jean-Pierre Duquette says that "the relations between objects and beings, the way in which we perceive things are crucial to Flaubert's way of expressing the real" (*Flaubert ou l'architecture du vide: Une lecture de L'Education sentimentale* [Montreal: Les Presses de l'Université de Montréal, 1972], 15). *L'Education* does not show the epistemological drama of consciousness grappling with reality. These descriptive passages represent perception, impressions, but these impressions are not causally connected nor are they "objective correlatives" for the character's interior states. In Flaubert's texts we see an oscillation between a character's alienation from and fusion with matter—e.g., the famous ending of *La Tentation de Saint Antoine*, "être la matière."

The tension between action and description appears in verb tenses. After reading that Frédéric and Rosanette "walked over some big rocks and soon came to the bottom of the gorge," the reader finds a new paragraph and the following description: "Elle est couverte, d'un côté, par un entremêlement de grès et de genevriers, tandis que, de l'autre, le terrain presque nu s'incline vers le creux du vallon ..." (323–24). (Baldick translates this in the past: "One side was covered with a jumble of sandstone rocks and junipers, while the other side, which was practically bare, sloped down to the trough of the valley ..." [321].) The present puts into relief the "action" of the objects during the time of Frédéric's visit. (See 325, 323, for another example.)

11. *The Gaze of Orpheus and Other Literary Essays,* trans. Lydia Davis, preface Geoffrey Hartman (Barrytown, NY: Station Hill, 1981), 130–31. The essay originally appeared in *Entretien infini* (Paris: Gallimard, 1969).

12. Obviously, there are many differences between Flaubert and Beckett; my purpose is only to wrench the reader from two kinds of intertexts that have dominated Flaubert criticism—Balzacian realism and the *nouveau roman.* For other juxtapositions of Flaubert and Beckett, see Shoshana Felman, "Modernité du lieu commun," in *La Folie et la chose littéraire* (Paris: Seuil, 1978), and Hugh Kenner, *The Stoic Comedians: Flaubert, Joyce, Beckett* (Berkeley: University of California Press, 1962).

13. Hamon says, "Historical or geographical proper names (Rouen, rue de Rivoli, Notre Dame de Paris, etc.), which refer to stable semantic entities that one must recognize as proper names—the capitalization is the differentiating typographical mark—more than understand, work a bit like citations from pedagogical discourse. They assure anchoring points, establish the performance (garants-auctores) of the referential statement by linking the text to valorized 'outside-text,' permit the economy of the descriptive statement and assure the global 'effet de réel' that transcends all details . . ." (426).

14. *L'Idiot de la famille* (Paris: Gallimard, 1971), I, 635.

15. *La Nouvelle Revue Francaise* 14 (1920): 72–90.

CHAPTER 2

1. Flaubert, *Correspondance* (Paris: Gallimard, 1973–84), II, 585–86; Heidegger, *Being and Time,* 213.

2. In *Le Père Goriot* Rastignac finds that Vautrin's account of the nature of society and that of Mme de Beauséant are the same, even though the two initiators come from entirely different social strata. Lukács explains this agreement: "This profound conformity in the assessment of what is essential in capitalist reality, this conformity of opinion between the escaped convict and the flower of the aristocratic *intelligentsia* takes the place of the theatrically mystic appearance of Mephistopheles [in Goethe's *Faust*]," *Studies in European Realism,* trans. Edith Bone (London: Hillway, 1950), 62.

3. The cliché is a historical phenomenon that is best defined from the point of view of reception. Michael Riffaterre gives the following definition: "The cliche is taken to be a group of words that elicits reactions such as: déjà vu, banal, hackneyed, artificial elegance, worn out, fossilized, etc." ("Le Cliché dans la prose littéraire," in *Essais de stylistique structurale* [Paris: Flammarion, 1971], 162). The cliché "is of a structural not semantic order since the substitution of a synonym effaces the cliché" (162). Ruth Amossy and Elisheva Rosen define *lieu commun* as part of *inventio (topoi),* not part of *elocutio,* which is where clichés and tropes are situated. Thus *lieu commun* "is defined at the level of ideas and arguments and refers to a stereotype of thought and not to a discursive unity." Their example, which I must leave in French, clarifies this distinction: "La dépréciation de l'éphémère est un lieu commun, 'feu de paille' un cliché," *Les Discours du cliché* (Paris: CDU-SEDES, 1982), 13–14. Anne Herschberg-Pierrot makes an important qualification in "Problématiques du cliché," *Poétique* 43 (1980), where she distin-

guishes Aristotle's *topoi* and *lieu commun*. The former is merely a formal category, whereas the latter designates content (338). In *L'Education sentimentale, lieux communs (idées reçues)* are more important than clichés. Actual citations from historical or literary texts do not appear.

4. Balzac's novels use the cliché to criticize the existing ideology and not just to confirm it. Amossy and Rosen note:
> Beyond the modalities that produce the referential illusion, which criticism has recently explored, the hackneyed figure shows how Balzacian writing makes the best use of its nimble exploitation of the paradigmatic dimension of the text. As a textual element, the hackneyed figure takes on various functions depending on how one conceives of it on the syntagmatic level or the level of the associative series that come from textual paradigms. On the other hand, the worn-out figure contributes to the imposition of a meaning that conforms to the norms of a given society; on the other hand, this figure permits—thanks to the unedited semantic juxtapositions—a radical questioning of the dominant ideology." (65)

5. *Balzac and the Comedy of Words* (Princeton: Princeton University Press, 1975), 236.

6. "Le Dialogue dans l'oeuvre de Flaubert," *Europe* (1969): 115–16. She cites Flaubert's famous remark on dialogue: "Je trouve que le dialogue doit être *caractéristique*" (115). ["I think dialogue must be typical."]

7. See Hamon, "Un Discours contraint," for detailed examples.

8. At Frédéric's apartment the divergent arguments are halted by a call for the destruction of "l'ordre actuel." We read in an isolated paragraph, "Everyone applauded, especially Dussardier" (140; 145).

9. Groups are even given a voice. When "le peuple" takes the Tuileries, we read, "Puisqu'on était victorieux, ne fallait-il pas s'amuser?" (290). Baldick translates this: "They were the victors, so surely they were entitled to enjoy themselves" (289).

10. Claude Perruchot's fascinating article "*Madame Bovary* et la question du sujet," in *La Production du sens chez Flaubert*, ed. Claudine Gothot-Mersch (Paris: Union Générale d'éditions, 1975), shows how free indirect representation is informed not by the fusion of the voices of the narrator and the character nor by either of their individual voices. I need not enter into the details here since his line of reasoning is clear: "this style pierces the border between interior and exterior with so many holes that it [this border] disappears. FID does not bridge a gap even in grammar by crossing verbs of one person with complements of another. Rather, this style is the gap between persons, the margin between discourses, the discord between the tense of the adverbs and the verbs . . ." (261). For general studies of FID, see Dorrit Cohn, *Transparent Minds* (Princeton: Princeton University Press, 1978) and Brian McHale, "Free Indirect Discourse: A Survey of Recent Accounts," *PTL* (1978): 249–87. For studies of FID in Flaubert, see Stephen Ullman, *Style in the French Novel* (New York: Barnes and Noble, 1964) and Sterling Haig, *Flaubert and the Gift of Speech* (Cambridge: Cambridge University Press, 1986).

11. Dambreuse's advice to Frédéric on the water-power industry (189–90; 192–93) is an excellent example of the use of reported speech, FID and direct quotation. Dambreuse wants to present the economic and political condi-

tions in such a way that Frédéric will be persuaded to accept a position with the company. (See Pierre Cogny, *L'Education sentimentale: Ou le monde en creux* [Paris: Larousse, 1975], 123–28, for the thematic importance of the passage.)

12. Claudine Gothot-Mersch notes, "Flaubert's characters all speak the same language: in content, they utter clichés that they have in common with many people; in style, the characters speak 'a classical language with few individual variations. We are very far from the variety of a great creator of dialogue such as Proust" (117). Flaubert's manuscripts reveal that he suppressed examples of "real" speech and replaced them with grammatically correct formal speech.

13. *The Family Idiot*, trans. Carol Cosman (Chicago: University of Chicago Press, 1981), 596.

14. Another example of this use of argumentative links in FID is: "Il [Frédéric] se sentait le coeur dur comme la table où ses coudes posaient. *Donc*, il pouvait, maintenant, se jeter au milieu du monde, sans peur" (109). ("He felt as if his heart was as hard as the table on which his elbows were resting. Now he could throw himself into society life without fear" [117].) The narrator's transitions almost always note only temporal ("puis", "alors") or additive ("et") space between events, never a causal or argumentative connection. For example, in the next sentence the thought of Deslauriers interrupts the logical development of Frédéric's ideas: "L'idée des Dambreuse lui vint; il les utiliserait; puis il se rappela Deslauriers" (109). ("He thought of the Dambreuses; he would make use of them; then he remembered Deslauriers" [117].) These argumentative links often appear in the free indirect representation of speech as well as thought: "Pellerin n'admettait pas qu'il y eût de belles femmes (il préférait les tigres); d'ailleurs, la femelle de l'homme était une créature inférieure dans la hiérarchie esthétique" (57). ("Pellerin refused to admit that there were any beautiful women [he preferred tigers]; besides, the human female was an inferior creature in the aesthetic hierarchy" [67].)

15. "Naturellement" appears fourteen times in the novel, frequently in reported speech.

16. *La Poétique de la rêverie* (Paris: Presses universitaires de France, 1974), 130.

CHAPTER 3

1. Roland Barthes, *S/Z*, 51; 44; Sartre, *L'Idiot*, II, 1176.
2. Other examples of commentary are:
   For some men, the stronger their desire, the more difficult it is for them to act. They are hampered by mistrust of themselves, daunted by the fear of causing offence; besides, deep feelings of affection are like respectable women; they are afraid of being found out and go through life with downcast eyes. (171; 174)

   For there are situations in which the kindest of men is so detached from his fellows that he would watch the whole human race perish without batting an eye. (285; 283)

Frédéric, accustomed to the affected grimaces of provincial housewives, had never seen such ease of manner in any woman, not that studied simplicity which the ingenuous regard as a sign of immediate sympathy. (89; 98)

For in the midst of the most intimate confidences, false shame, delicacy, or pity always impose a certain reticence. We come across precipices or morasses, in ourselves or in the other person, which bring us to a halt; in any case, we feel that we would not be understood; it is difficult to express anything at all with any degree of exactness, so that complete relationships are few and far between. (331–32; 328)

3. *Correspondance* (Paris: Gallimard, 1973–84), I, 678–79.

4. In what is now a cliché of Flaubert criticism, Barthes says, "Flaubert . . . using an irony fraught with uncertainty, achieves a salutary malaise of writing: he does not stop the play of codes (or stops it partially), so that (and this is indubitably of the *proof* of writing) *one never knows if he is responsible for what he writes* (if there is a subject *behind* his language; for the very being of writing (the meaning of the labor that constitutes it) is to keep the question *Who is speaking?* from ever being answered") (146). This quote does not mean that the narrator's presence is a nonpositioned subject who is withheld from the reader—as Flaubert wants to have it in the quote from the *Correspondance*—but a multipositioned subject. See Sartre's account of *le survol*, Flaubert's attempt to rise above humanity—and positionality—in successive "upward" movements (*L'Idiot*, II, 1180–85).

5. In *Histoire et langage dans L'Education sentimentale*, ed. Maurice Agulhon et al. (Paris: SEDES, 1981).

6. The language used to represent the people in the passage that Herschberg-Pierrot analyzes is pejorative (e.g., "la canaille," 290). Pejorative language appears in the representation of all social groups and its appearance raises questions about the authority of the speaker's voice. One of the most interesting passages appears in the portrait of Sénécal: "He was familiar with Mably, Morelly, Fourier, Saint-Simon, Comte, Cabet, Louis Blanc, the whole cartload of Socialist writers *(la lourde charretée des écrivains socialistes)*—those who wanted to reduce mankind to the level of the barrackroom, send it to the brothel for its amusement, and tie it to the counter or bench" (136–37; 141). The emphasized phrase invokes our knowledge of socialist writers, effaces differences among them, points to their stylistic deficiencies and utopian fantasies, and assumes that we also make such judgments.

7. "Assumed knowledge" is what Barthes calls "le code gnomique" (*S/Z* [Paris: Seuil, 1970], 25) and what Chatman calls "deictic lubrication" (*Story and Discourse* [Ithaca: Cornell University Press, 1978], 246–47). Some other examples of the use of assumed knowledge are: ". . . she was in that carefree mood which is characteristic of great happiness" (273; 271–72); "Frédéric felt the sort of surprise one experiences when one sees a practical joke brought off successfully" (76; 85); "When she had been a little girl, she had conceived one of those childish passions which combine both the purity of a religion and the violence of desire" (251; 250–51).

8. *Le Plaisir du texte* (Paris: Seuil, 1973), 69.

9. *Gustave Flaubert* (Paris: Gallimard, 1935), 265.

144 NOTES

10. I shall present my theory of metaphor in my analysis of *The Golden Bowl*, a novel that exploits its possibilities. See Chapter 7.

11. They note that verisimilitude in the realistic novel demands that the comparison avoid two complementary dangers that threaten the "transparence" necessary to realism: 1. "the dated trope," 2. "the unsettling discovery" (70). Although realistic discourse may be disturbed by "unusual" language that calls attention to itself the forces of reference are not incompatible with such language.

12. Some other examples of comparisons are:
He felt as doomed as a man who has fallen into a chasm where he knows that no help will come and he is going to die. (200; 202)

Beside her, he felt less important on earth than the scraps of silk which fell from her scissors. (171; 174)

... he no longer felt anything but an immense, pleasantly stupid well-being, like a plant saturated with heat and moisture. (112; 119)

13. Since the novel concentrates on the protagonist, the problem of the textual forces and the hero overlap. I limit myself to an analysis of the narratological features of the novel and irony in this chapter and discuss Frédéric's experience in the next.

14. *Figures III* (Paris: Seuil, 1972), 131. *Récit* and *histoire* are Genette's terms from "Discours du récit" (in *Figures III*), while discourse and story are Chatman's corresponding English terms in *Story and Discourse*. Chatman provides the following definitions: "Story is the content of the narrative expression, while discourse is the form of the expression" (*Story and Discourse*, 23). For a discussion of the presuppositions of and problems with this opposition, see my essay "The Dangers of Structuralist Narratology: Genette's Misinterpretation of Proust," *Romance Notes* 26 (1986): 1–7.

15. In "Le Rôle du hasard dans *L'Education sentimentale*," *Europe* (1969): 101–7, Jean Bruneau cites nearly forty examples. He concludes that "the motor of the novel is chance, both in the succession of events as in the meetings of the characters" (106).

16. *Anatomy of Criticism* (Princeton: Princeton University Press, 1957), 34.

17. In speaking of Kafka and Joyce, Frye notes how the ironic moves from "realism and dispassionate observation" toward myth. See *Anatomy*, 41–43.

CHAPTER 4

1. The extraordinary precision of these details has attracted the attention of Gérard Genette: "The precision of the details—particularly the last—goes beyond the verisimilitude of pretext. One of the most distinctive aspects of Flaubert's writing is this excess of material presence in supposedly subjective scenes, where verisimilitude would call for vague, diffuse, ungraspable evocations" ("Les Silences de Flaubert," *Figures I* [Paris: Seuil, 1966], 226). Genette goes on to explain these breaks in verisimilitude by Flaubert's love of contemplation and praises the way such passages (and much of Flaubert's description) resist motivation by reference to the psychol-

ogy of the character or the setting. From my point of view, what is important is the ontological liberation that these reveries represent.

2. In a letter to Taine, Flaubert explains: "The interior life of the artist resembles the fugacity of hypnogogic hallucinations, which pass before your eyes. That is the moment when one must eagerly leap right in" (*Correspondance inédite. Supplément*, 4 vols. [Paris: Conard, 1954], II, 93). The last sentence of their meeting at the end of the novel is: "Et ce fut tout" (423); ("And that was all" [416]).

3. Moreover, this paragraph, like the one cited above, ends with a word that points beyond language into a semantic space between paragraphs ("pas de limites", "infini"). Occasionally such sentences end with a syntactically unusual adverb: "la tente de coutil formait un large dais sur sa tête, et les petits glands rouges de la bordure tremblaient à la brise, perpétuellement" (9) ("the drill awning forming a wide canopy over her head, and the little red tassels on the fringe trembling perpetually in the breeze" [22]).

4. Richard, *Littérature et sensation* (Paris: Seuil, 1954), 215.

5. See Michal Peled Ginsburg, *Flaubert Writing* (Palo Alto: Stanford University Press, 1986), for the way metonymy generates the plot of *L'Education*.

6. In *Oh les beaux jours*, Winnie makes a similar attempt to surmount the present. The prayers with which she opens Acts I and II are much like the hymn of romantic platitudes that Frédéric recites to Madame Arnoux in this scene. Both are attempts to break the weight of the present reality.

CHAPTER 5

1. *The Art of the Novel*, ed. R. P. Blackmur (New York: Scribners, 1934), 46. This work will be designated *AN* in the text.

2. *Literary Criticism: Essays on Literature*, 50.

3. *The Princeton Encyclopedia of Poetry and Poetics* (Princeton: Princeton University Press, 1974), 363. See Paul Armstrong's *The Phenomenology of Henry James* (Chapel Hill: University of North Carolina Press, 1983), which criticizes the empiricist reading of James's texts and explores their phenomenological dimensions.

4. *The Political Unconscious* (Ithaca: Cornell University Press, 1982), 224. Two recent examples of James criticism that use the opposition between subject and object are Alfred Habegger's *Gender, Fantasy, and Realism in American Literature* (New York: Columbia University Press, 1982) and Ralf Norrman's *The Insecure World of Henry James's Fiction* (New York: St. Martin's, 1982). Habegger says that "James's profound solipsistic tendencies hindered his powers of observation" (277). Norrman discusses the relationship of language and reality: "One way to ensure that language has power over reality is to see to it that whatever has been imagined verbally is never checked against reality" (130). John Carlos Rowe's chapter "Literary *Impressionism*," in *The Theoretical Dimensions of Henry James* (Madison: University of Wisconsin Press, 1984), shows that "there are no impressions that are not always involved in semantic and social historical determinations" (194). This Derridean insight is the point of departure for my analysis of the semantic space of the impression.

5. The text's symbolism, e.g., the golden bowl, is not an englobing meaning imposed from the outside by the narrator or the author; it is taken up by the characters. That is, myth and symbols are part of the stories that the characters make up about each other and not part of an ultimate language intended only for the reader.

6. In Balzac setting is established in realistic discourse and connected with the characters so that they are constrained by their social and physical surroundings. As we saw earlier, an understanding of Mme de Bargeton requires information on Angoulême: "it is all the more necessary at this point to make some remarks on Angoulême because they will help us to understand Madame de Bargeton, one of the most important characters in this story" (64; 31).

7. A. J. Greimas and J. Courtés define disengagement or *débrayage* as follows: "the operation by which the domain of the enunciation disjuncts and projects forth from itself, at the moment of the language act and in view of manifestation, certain terms bound to its base structure, so as thereby to constitute the foundational elements of the discourse-utterance," *Semiotics and Language*, trans. Larry Crist et al. (Bloomington: Indiana University Press, 1982), 87.

8. "Texte, référence, déictique," *Texte*, 1 (1982): 122.

9. Greimas, 102.

10. Seymour Chatman, *The Later Style of Henry James* (Oxford: Blackwell, 1972), 50.

11. We never learn precisely what Charlotte wears, only that her clothes "were simply the most charming and interesting that any woman had ever put on" (II, 13).

12. The portrait of Fanny is a comic version of this metaphorical creation of character: "Full of discriminations against the obvious, she had yet to accept a flagrant appearance and to make the best of misleading signs. Her richness of hue, her generous nose, her eyebrows marked like those of an actress—these things, with an added amplitude of person on which middle age had set its seal, seemed to present her insistently as a daughter of the South, or still more of the East, a creature formed by hammocks and divans, fed upon sherbets and waited upon by slaves" (I, 34).

13. After announcing—impulsively and somewhat gratuitously—to Maria that he is from Woollett, Strether demonstrates his self-consciousness: " 'Oh I think it's a thing,' he said, 'that you must already have made out. I feel it so that I certainly must look it, speak it, and, as people say there, 'act' it' " (*The Ambassadors* [New York: Scribners, 1909], I, 15).

14. "He [the Prince] had an idea—which may amuse his historian—that when you were stupid enough to be mistaken about such a matter you did know it" (I, 17). The Prince's confidence in his powers of discernment is emphasized throughout the text. When Charlotte says, "we may perish by cracks in things that we don't know," Amerigo replies: " 'Ah, but one does know. I do at least—and by instinct. I don't fail. That will always protect me' " (I, 119–20). He is also quick to accuse others of "failures of wit" when they fall out with him. When Fanny refuses to understand his relationship with Charlotte, he thinks, "they came to the same thing, all such collapses . . . , the failure of wit" (I, 314). He even accuses Charlotte of "stupidity" in Book II (II, 348). The Prince's smugness about knowledge is related to

his treatment of all people as things, from "liking them almost as if he collected them, in the manner of book-plates or postage stamps, for themselves . . ." (I, 160–61). He turns Charlotte into a work of art (I, 45–46), tries to find their excursion only "amusing" and accepts Adam's and Maggie's classification of him as "a *morceau de musée*" (I, 12).

15. There are examples of this vocabulary of concepts throughout his work. In *The Portrait of a Lady* (New York: Scribners, 1909), we read, "Isabel had spoken to him [Ralph Touchett] very often about 'specimens'; it was a word that played a considerable part in her vocabulary; she wished him to understand that she wished to see English society illustrated by eminent cases" (I, 89). Of Milly Teale in *The Wings of the Dove* (New York: Scribners, 1909), we read, "she *knew* the three [women at the National Gallery] generically as a school-boy with a crib in his lap would know the answer in class" (I, 290–91).

16. *The Ambassadors* also thematizes the impossibility of exiling the "vulgarity" of history and economics—from the comic play with the unnamed item of manufacture to Chad's move into advertising. See Mark Seltzer's *Henry James and the Art of Power* (Ithaca: Cornell University Press, 1984) for a Foucaldian analysis of the complicity between the Jamesian text and the discourses of power and discipline.

CHAPTER 6

1. Preface to *The Golden Bowl*, xxiv.
2. *Poétique de la prose* (Paris: Seuil, 1971), 153.
3. Henry James, ed., *The Letters of William James*, 2 vols. (Boston: Atlantic Monthly Press, 1920), II, 278.
4. For a subtle discussion of James's dialogues and attempts to categorize them, see Yeazell's chapter "Talking in James." My reading seeks to establish the philosophical motor of the dialogues rather than offer thematic or psychological readings.
5. John Searle, *Speech Acts* (Cambridge: Cambridge University Press, 1969), 79.
6. J. L. Austin, *How to Do Things with Words*, 2nd ed., ed. J. O. Urmson and Marina Sbisa (Cambridge: Harvard University Press, 1975).
7. Derrida explores the power of citation: "Every sign, linguistic or nonlinguistic, spoken or written (in the usual sense of this opposition), as a small or large unity, can be *cited*, put between quotation marks; thereby it can break with every given context, and engender infinitely new contexts in an absolutely nonsaturable fashion. This does not suppose that the mark is valid outside its context, but on the contrary that there are only contexts without any center of absolute anchoring. This citationality, duplication, or duplicity, this iterability of the mark is not an accident or an anomaly, but is that (normal/abnormal) without which a mark could no longer even have a so-called "normal" functioning" ("Signature Event Context," in *Margins of Philosophy*, trans. Alan Bass [Chicago: University of Chicago Press, 1982], 320–21).
8. The use of demonstratives in this passage can be clarified by a glance at Bertrand Russell's celebrated discussion. Though I do not subscribe to his

theory of acquaintance and its perceptual grounding, the following citation illustrates the tension between signification and reference and the disruptive force that reference to a new entity can create for speakers:

> When we use the word "Socrates," we are really using a description. Our thought may be rendered by some phrase such as, "The Master of Plato" or "The philosopher who drank the hemlock" ... but we certainly do not use the name as a name in the proper sense of the word. [Thus] the only words one does use as names in the logical sense are words like "this" or "that." One can use "this" as a name to stand for a particular with which one is acquainted at the moment. We say, "This is white." If you agree "This is white," meaning "this" that you see, you are using "this" as a proper name. But if you try to apprehend the proposition that I am expressing when I say "This is white," you cannot do it. If you mean this piece of chalk as a physical object, then you are not using a proper name. It is only when you use "this" quite strictly, to stand for an actual object of sense, that it is a proper name. And in that it has a very odd property for a proper name, namely that it seldom means the same thing two moments running and does not mean the same thing to the speaker and the hearer ("The Philosophy of Logical Atomism," in *Logic and Knowledge* [London: George Allen and Unwin, 1956], 201).

9. Maggie uses a similar strategy in Volume II through her insistence on the details of the Prince's two excursions (to Gloucester and to the art dealer) and through her references to her own speeches. The narrator gives a marvelous account of these processes in the penultimate chapter: "They [her ideas] were all, apparently queer for him, but she had at least with the lapse of months created the perception that there might be something in them; whereby he stared there, beautiful and sombre, at what she was at present providing him with. There was something of his own in his mind to which she was sure he referred everything for a measure and a meaning; he had never let go of it from the evening, weeks before, when, in her room after his encounter with the Bloomsbury cup, she had planted it there by flinging it at him, on the question of her father's view of him, her determined 'Find out for yourself!' " (II, 344).

10. The reversibility of art and life is suggested in Maggie's conceptions of herself as an actress (II, 33; II, 208; II, 33), a circus performer (II, 302), and as a playwright: "they might have been figures rehearsing some play of which she herself was the author" (II, 235). The narrator employs the metaphor of text: "and, in respect to the rest of the whole matter of her obligation to follow her husband, that personage and she, Maggie, had so shuffled away every link between consequence and cause, that the intention remained, like some famous line in a dead language, subject to varieties of interpretation" (II, 345).

11. "L'Art des pronoms et le nommé dans l'oeuvre de Nathalie Sarraute," *Romanic Review* 72 (1981): 207.

12. The difficulties in discussing the relationships among language, thought and being can be seen in Benveniste's attempt to derive thought from language. His discussion of Aristotle's concept of being provides a foil to my discussion: "Without being a predicate itself, being is the condition of all predicates" (Catégories de pensée et catégories de langue," in *Problèmes*

de linguistique générale [Paris: Gallimard, 1966], I, 70). Derrida—using Heidegger's study of being in *Introduction to Metaphysics*—unveils problems in Benveniste's essay in "Supplément de copule," in *Margins of Philosophy*. Through stylistic analysis, my reading of *The Golden Bowl* takes up this challenge made to realistic ontology. See Chapter 7.

13. In Norrman's *The Insecure World of Henry James*, there is an excellent chapter, "Referential Ambiguity in Pronouns," on the use of personal pronouns in dialogue: "The act of adultery is focused in pronouns. The Prince and Charlotte have to commit a pronominal union first, and this is the real point at which they slip into sin; the fact will follow" (24). However, he reduces the role of pronouns to ambiguity and intensity: "the main role of referential ambiguity" is "to function as a dramatization of the combinations and thereby create intensity" (15). Hence, he reads this scene in an amazingly realistic fashion. The talk about the bowl is just a screen for real motives, the real "what" of the situation: "The Prince wanted to give Charlotte a present as a small *ricordo*, which gives Charlotte the chance to make her refusal a pretext to get closer still to the real subject; their relationship with each other. It would be a *ricordo* of nothing, since they have not as yet shared any experience worth commemorating" (93).

CHAPTER 7

1. *Figures II* (Paris: Seuil, 1969), 79–80.
2. "The verisimilar narrative is therefore a narration whose actions correspond, as so many applications or particular cases to a body of maxims understood as true by the public to whom it is addressed" (*Figures II*, 76).
3. Chatman's "nonnarrated discourse" and Benveniste's "histoire," in which the speaker is effaced, depend on the *scripteur's* (author's) submission to a received language of representation.
4. Another example of the narrator's separation of Maggie's feelings from the vocabulary of realism comes after several metaphors that try to locate the heroine's emotional "place" without regard to the Prince: "Maggie's own [place], in short, would have been sought in vain in the most rudimentary map of the social relations as such. The only geography marking it would be doubtless that of the fundamental passions" (II, 324).
5. Cited in Mark Johnson, ed., *Philosophical Perspectives on Metaphor* (Minneapolis: University of Minnesota Press, 1981), 16.
6. See Derrida's essay "De l'économie restreinte à l'économie générale," in *L'Ecriture et la différence* (Paris: Seuil, 1967), where he opposes the restricted economy of logocentrism with the general economy of writing.
7. See Emile Benveniste's discussion of the aorist in *Problèmes de linguistique générale* (Paris: Gallimard, 1966), I, 225–57.
8. "Consciousness" itself becomes a metaphor for an interior territory that Maggie explores—i.e., that surpasses her consciousness in the conven-

tional sense: "Maggie inwardly lived in a consciousness that she could but partly open even to so good a friend and her own visitation of the fuller expanse of which was for that matter still going on" (II, 219).

9. The narrator does this in other places as well: "Something of this sort was in any case the moral and the murmur of his walk" (I, 18).

10. "High" is an intensifier that usually modifies a state by indicating that this state partakes of the sublime and that this sublimity is achieved only by a remarkable transcendence (spatial metaphor) of divisive tensions. Other examples of this use of "high" are: I, 293; I, 296; I, 312; I, 330; II, 71.

11. My theory of metaphor—which I am not distinguishing from analogy—follows in part Paul Ricoeur's comprehensive treatment in *The Rule of Metaphor*. Ricoeur distinguishes three levels of the metaphoric enunciation: "the tension between the terms of the statement, the tension between literal interpretation and metaphorical interpretation, and the tension in the reference between is and is not" (298). This analysis yields two levels of signification: "the first meaning relates to a known field of reference, that is to the sphere of entities to which the predicates considered in their established meaning can be attached. The second meaning, the one that is to be made apparent, relates to a referential field for which there is no direct characterization, for which we consequently are unable to make identifying descriptions by means of appropriate predicates" (299). However, I do not agree with Ricoeur's distinctions between philosophical and poetic metaphors and between literary and nonliterary texts. For metaphor in the texts of philosophy, see Derrida's "The White Mythology," in *Margins of Philosophy*.

12. Roland Barthes, "Proust et les noms," in *Les Critiques de notre temps*, ed. Jacques Bersani (Paris: Garnier, 1971), 160. Unlike *A la recherche*, *The Golden Bowl* emphasizes the discontinuity of names and metaphors rather than their capacity to create essences.

13. Some other examples: "That figure has however a freedom for us that the occasion doubtless scarce demands, though we may retain it for its rough negative value" (I, 197); "or call it even if one would a house of cards" (II, 81); "for which Maggie suspected fundamentals, as I have called them" (II, 78).

14. *Henry James: The Major Phase* (New York: Oxford University Press, 1963), 22–23.

15. *Transparent Minds* (Princeton: Princeton University Press, 1978), 43.

16. Jean-François Lyotard defines postmodernism as "incredulity toward metanarrative" in *The Postmodern Condition*, trans. Geoff Bennington and Brian Massumi (Minneapolis: University of Minnesota Press, 1984), xxiv. The Jamesian text illustrates the way characters construct conflicting narratives of what has taken place. The narrator does not reconcile these conflicts with an all-embracing story that brings the work to closure.

17. For Chatman, these stylistic features do not alter the ontology of the text. James's novels simply "foreground" (35) or "emphasize" certain elements with regard to other texts. (Chatman uses four contemporary novels for comparison: Gissing's *Veranilda* [1905], Forster's *Where Angels Fear to Tread* [1905], Butler's *The Way of All Flesh* [1904], and Conrad's *Typhoon* [1902].) In addition, Chatman does not treat reference. Even deixis is defined only intralinguistically: "Deixis is usually defined as backward reference" [i.e., to another term] (62). Metaphor is simply a device that is explained

genetically: "It is as if the loss of contact with the physical world that James's preoccupation with abstractions and the inner life entailed was to be recaptured in metaphor" (111). Chatman's universalist view of literary history is perhaps supported by his commitment to Chomsky's universal grammar. Ian Hacking discusses the relationship of grammatical conceptions to conceptions of the mind and the world:
> One answer, that of Russell and Davidson, leads to the view that the substance-attribute metaphysic is derived from a mistaken grammatical theory, which is strong, though not conclusive reason for saying it is wrong. Another answer, that of the followers of Chomsky, is that the basic, ancient, grammatical hunch was right. That can only help restore the substance-attribute metaphysics." (*Why Does Language Matter to Philosophy* [Cambridge: Cambridge University Press, 1975], 91–92)

For transformational grammar, James's stylistic features—like those of any text—are surface changes of deep structures common to all texts.

18. Chatman says that "the 'clefting' transformation performs either of the following two operations: either it places *what* before the noun phrase and *be* between the verb and its object: 'coughs cause disease'—'what causes coughs is disease'; or it replaces the subject with *what* and adds the subject at the end, after an inserted *be:* 'Coughs cause disease'—'what causes diseases is coughs' " (64). "It" can be used instead of "what" in cleft constructions.

19. These structures can also be found in *The Ambassadors:* "[H]ere was something for his [Strether's] problem . . . that floated in upon him as if part of a sudden flood" (II, 149); "What carried Strether hither and yon was an admirable theory . . ." (I, 76); "Nothing could have been odder than Strether's sense of himself as at that moment launched into something of which the sense would be quite disconnected from the sense of his past and which was literally beginning there and then" (I, 9); "the thing indeed really unmistakeable was its rolling over him as a wave that he had been, in conditions incalculable and unimaginable, a subject of discussion" (I, 212).

20. "Causes" appear elsewhere as an element of poetic plenitude rather than as a logical connection: "it would have been all indescribably remarkable, this fact that, with wonderful causes for it so operating on the surface, nobody else, as yet, in the combination, seemed estranged from anybody" (I, 315).

21. The purpose of the analogy is to represent the nature of their relationship, not their evolution. The temporal aspect of the figure—the movement of the carriage on the road—is not disruptive; hence, time is implicitly circular.

22. The "present situation" is dominated by the Ververs and represented from the Prince's point of view. Even though the Prince feels exiled from the Americans, he is not ready to leave them and join Charlotte.

23. *Literary Criticism: Essays on Literature*, 1403.

24. The organization of the text around a referent also appears in *The Ambassadors*. See the examples of Maria's band (I, 50–53), Paris (I, 88–93), and Chad's appearance (I, 134–43).

25. Other uses of the word "play" are: I, 33; I, 34; I, 67; I, 68; I, 157; II, 35; II, 84; II, 180; II, 235; II, 365.

26. *Critique of Judgment*, trans. J. H. Bernard (New York: Haffner Press, 1951), 65.

27. In *The Ambassadors* the role of aesthetic values in expanding Strether's referential and ethical horizons is foregrounded, while in *The Golden Bowl* the crippling effect of facile play is emphasized.

28. The narrator intervenes explicitly in the presentation of Adam: "Nothing perhaps might affect us as queerer, had we time to look into it, than this application of the same measure of value to such different pieces of property as old Persian carpets, say, and new human acquisitions" (I, 196). "It was all at bottom in him, the aesthetic principle, planted where it could burn with a cold still flame; where it fed almost wholly on the material directly involved, on the idea (followed by appropriation) of plastic beauty, of the thing visibly perfect in its kind" (I, 197). Adam has a revelation about his affinity with grand collectors and even artists: "[N]ow he read into his career, in one single magnificent night, the immense meaning it had waited for" (I, 142).

CHAPTER 8

1. *A la recherche du temps perdu* (Paris: Gallimard, 1954), III, 519.

2. Early in the novel, Fanny declares: " 'She [Maggie] wasn't born to know evil. She must never know it' " (I, 78).

3. The Prince notes and approves of Maggie's treatment of guests as objects: "Only Maggie herself had her own odd way—which didn't moreover the least irritate him—of really liking them [guests] in proportion as they could strike her as strange. It came out in her by heredity, he amused himself with declaring, this love of *chinoiseries*" (I, 162).

4. Maggie reaffirms the value of this knowledge: " 'I put him in possession of the difference; the difference made about me by the fact that I hadn't been after all . . . too stupid to have arrived at knowledge. He had to see that I'm changed for him—quite changed from the idea of me that he had so long been going on with. It became a question then of his really taking in the change—and what I now see is that he's doing so' " (II, 216).

5. Maggie's earlier attempt to figure this relationship is filled with confused images: "There had been, through life, as we know, few quarters in which the Princess's fancy could let itself loose; but it shook off restraint when it plunged into the figured void of the detail of that relation. This was a realm it could people with images—again and again with fresh ones; they swarmed there like the strange combinations that lurked in the woods at twilight" (II, 280).

6. Having distinguished judgment about final causes from knowledge in *The Critique of Pure Reason*, Kant discusses the function of purposiveness for aesthetic judgment in the third moment of *The Critique of Judgment*: "The consciousness of the mere formal purposiveness in the play of the subject's cognitive powers, in a representation through which an object is given, is the pleasure itself, because it contains a determining ground of the activity of the subject in respect of the excitement of its cognitive powers, and therefore an inner causality (which is purposive) in respect to cognition in general, without being limited to any definite cognition, and conse-

quently contains a mere form of the subjective purposiveness of a representation in an aesthetical judgment" (58). I do not want to deny that Maggie discovers new things in Volume II. I emphasize the way that she names them and the link between her teleological reading of events and her aesthetic reading of individuals. See Yeazell's book—which uses as its epigraph: "Knowledge, knowledge, was a fascination as well as a fear" (II, 140)—for a fine discussion of Maggie's ambivalence toward knowledge.

Works Cited

Agulhon, Maurice, et al., eds. *Histoire et langage dans L'Education sentimentale.* Paris: SEDES, 1981.
Altieri, Charles. *Act and Quality: A Theory of Meaning and Humanistic Understanding.* Amherst: University of Massachusetts Press, 1981.
Amossy, Ruth, and Elisheva Rosen. *Les Discours du cliché.* Paris: CDU-SEDES, 1982.
Armstrong, Paul. *The Phenomenology of Henry James.* Chapel Hill: University of North Carolina Press, 1983.
Auerbach, Erich. *Mimesis: The Representation of Reality in Western Literature.* Trans. Willard Trask. Garden City: Doubleday, 1957.
Austin, J. L. *How to Do Things with Words.* 2nd ed. Ed. J. O. Urmonson and Marina Sbisa. Cambridge: Harvard University Press, 1975.
Bachelard, Gaston. *La Poétique de la rêverie.* Paris: Presses universitaires de France, 1974.
Balzac, Honoré de. *Les Illusions perdues.* Paris: Garnier-Flammarion, 1966.
———. *Lost Illusions.* Trans. Herbert J. Hunt. New York: Penguin, 1971.
Barthes, Roland. "L'Effet de réel." *Communications* 11 (1968): 84–89.
———. *Essais critiques.* Paris: Seuil, 1964.
———. *Le Plaisir du texte.* Paris: Seuil, 1973.
———. *S/Z.* Paris: Seuil, 1970.
Benveniste, Emile. *Problèmes de linguistique générale.* 2 vols. Paris: Gallimard, 1966–74.
Bersani, Jacques, ed. *Les Critiques de notre temps.* Paris: Garnier, 1971.
Blanchot, Maurice. *L'Entretien infini.* Paris: Gallimard, 1969.
———. *The Gaze of Orpheus and Other Literary Essays.* Trans. Lydia Davis. Barrytown, NY: Station Hill, 1981.

156 WORKS CITED

Brombert, Victor. *The Novels of Flaubert: A Study of Themes and Techniques*. Princeton: Princeton University Press, 1966.
Brooks, Peter. *The Melodramatic Imagination: Balzac, Henry James, Melodrama and the Mode of Excess*. New Haven: Yale University Press, 1976.
Brown, Marshall. "The Logic of Realism: A Hegelian Approach." *PMLA* 96 (1981): 224–41.
Bruneau, Jean. "Le Rôle du hasard dans *L'Education sentimentale*." *Europe* (1969): 101–7.
Carroll, David. *The Subject in Question*. Chicago: University of Chicago Press, 1982.
Chatman, Seymour. *The Later Style of Henry James*. Oxford: Blackwell, 1972.
———. *Story and Discourse: Narrative Structure in Fiction and Film*. Ithaca: Cornell University Press, 1978.
Cogny, Pierre. *L'Education sentimentale de Flaubert ou le monde en creux*. Paris: Larousse, 1975.
Cohn, Dorrit. *Transparent Minds: Narrative Modes for Presenting Consciousness in Fiction*. Princeton: Princeton University Press, 1978.
Culler, Jonathan. *Flaubert: The Uses of Uncertainty*. London: Elek Books, 1974.
———. *On Deconstruction: Theory and Criticism After Structuralism*. Ithaca: Cornell University Press, 1982.
———. *Structuralist Poetics: Structuralism, Linguistics, and the Study of Literature*. Ithaca: Cornell University Press, 1975.
Davidson, Donald. "On the Very Idea of a Conceptual Scheme." *The Proceedings of the American Philosophical Association* 47 (1973–74): 5–20.
De Man, Paul. *Blindness and Insight: Essays in the Rhetoric of Contemporary Criticism*. 2nd ed. revised. Minneapolis: University of Minnesota Press, 1982.
———. "The Epistemology of Metaphor." *Critical Inquiry* 5 (1978): 13–30.
———. *The Resistance to Theory*. Minneapolis: University of Minnesota Press, 1986.
Derrida, Jacques. *L'Ecriture et la différence*. Paris: Seuil, 1967.
———. *Margins of Philosophy*. Trans. Alan Bass. Chicago: University of Chicago Press, 1982.
———. *Positions*. Trans. Alan Bass. Chicago: University of Chicago Press, 1981.
———. *La Voix et le phénomène*. Paris: Presses universitaires de France, 1967.
Dumesnil, René. *L'Education sentimentale de Gustave Flaubert*. Paris: Nizet, 1963.
Dummett, Michael. *Frege: Philosophy of Language*. London: Duckworth, 1973.
Duquette, Jean-Pierre. *Flaubert ou l'architecture du vide: Une lecture de l'Education sentimentale*. Montreal: Les Presses de l'université de Montréal, 1972.
Eco, Umberto. *Semiotics and the Philosophy of Language*. Bloomington: Indiana University Press, 1984.

Edwards, Paul, et al., eds. *Encyclopedia of Philosophy*. 8 vols. New York: Macmillan, 1967.
Felman, Shoshana. *La Folie et la chose littéraire*. Paris: Seuil, 1978.
Flaubert, Gustave. *Correspondance*. 2 vols. Paris: Gallimard, 1973–84.
———. *Correspondance inédite. Supplément*. 4 vols. Paris: Conard, 1954.
———. *L'Education sentimentale: Histoire d'un jeune homme*. Paris: Garnier Frères, 1964.
———. *The Sentimental Education*. Trans. Robert Baldick. New York: Penguin, 1964.
Frege, Gottlob. "Uber Sinn und Bedeutung." *Zeitschrift für Philosophie und philosophische Kritik* 100 (1892): 25–50.
———. *Translations from the Philosophical Writings of Gottlob Frege*. Trans. P. T. Geach and Max Black. Oxford: Blackwell, 1970.
Frye, Northrop. *Anatomy of Criticism: Four Essays*. Princeton: Princeton University Press, 1957.
Gadamer, Hans-Georg. *Truth and Method*. Trans. Garrett Barden and John Cumming. New York: Seabury Press, 1975.
Gale, Robert. *The Caught Image: Figurative Language in the Fiction of Henry James*. Chapel Hill: University of North Carolina Press, 1964.
Genette, Gérard. *Figures II*. Paris: Seuil, 1969.
———. *Figures III*. Paris: Seuil, 1972.
Gervais, David. *Flaubert and Henry James: A Study in Contrasts*. London: Macmillan, 1978.
Ginsburg, Michal Peled. *Flaubert Writing*. Palo Alto: Stanford University Press, 1986.
Goodman, Nelson. *The Ways of World Making*. Indianapolis: Hackett, 1978.
Gothot-Mersch, Claudine. "Le Dialogue dans l'oeuvre de Flaubert." *Europe* (1969): 112–21.
———, ed. *La Production du sens chez Flaubert*. Paris: Union générale d'éditions, 1975.
Graff, Gerald. *Literature Against Itself: Literary Ideas in Modern Society*. Chicago: University of Chicago Press, 1979.
Greimas, A. J., and J. Courtés. *Semiotics and Language*. Trans. Larry Crist et al. Bloomington: Indiana University Press, 1982.
Grover, Phillip. *Henry James and the French Novel: A Study in Inspiration*. London: Elek Books, 1973.
Habegger, Alfred. *Gender, Fantasy, and Realism in American Literature*. New York: Columbia University Press, 1982.
Hacking, Ian. *Why Does Language Matter to Philosophy?* Cambridge: Cambridge University Press, 1975.
Haig, Sterling. *Flaubert and the Gift of Writing*. Cambridge: Cambridge University Press, 1986.
Hamon, Philippe. "Un Discours contraint." *Poétique* 16 (1973): 411–45.
Heidegger, Martin. *Being and Time*. Trans. John Macquarrie and Edward Robinson. New York: Harper and Row, 1962.
———. *Early Greek Thinking*. Trans. David Farrell Krell and Frank Capuzzi. New York: Harper and Row, 1975.
———. *An Introduction to Metaphysics*. Trans. Ralph Mannheim. Garden City: Doubleday, 1961.

Herschberg-Pierrot, Anne. "Problématique du cliché." *Poétique* 43 (1980): 334–45.
James, Henry. *The Art of the Novel: Critical Prefaces by Henry James.* Ed. R. P. Blackmur. 1934. New York: Scribners, 1962.
———. *Literary Criticism: Essays on Literature, American Writers, English Writers.* New York: Library of America, 1984.
———. *Literary Criticism: French Writers, Other European Writers, The Prefaces to the New York Edition.* New York: Library of America, 1984.
———. *The Novels and Tales of Henry James.* The New York Edition. 24 vols. New York: Scribners, 1907–9.
James, William. *The Letters of William James.* Ed. Henry James. 2 vols. Boston: Atlantic Monthly Press, 1920.
Jameson, Frederic. *The Political Unconscious.* Ithaca: Cornell University Press, 1982.
Jay, Gregory. Review of *The Skeptic Disposition in Contemporary Culture*, by Eugene Goodheart. *Genre* 18 (1986): 297–303.
Johnson, Mark, ed. *Philosophical Perspectives on Metaphor.* Minneapolis: University of Minnesota Press, 1981.
Jost, François. "La Tradition du *Bildungsroman.*" *Comparative Literature* 21 (1969): 97–115.
Kadish, Doris. "Two Semiological Features of Four Functions of Descriptions: The Example of Flaubert." *Romanic Review* 69 (1979): 278–98.
Kanes, Martin. *Balzac and the Comedy of Words.* Princeton: Princeton University Press, 1975.
Kant, Immanuel. *Critique of Judgement.* Trans. J. H. Bernard. New York: Haffner Press, 1951.
Kenner, Hugh. *The Stoic Comedians: Flaubert, Joyce, Beckett.* Berkeley: University of California Press, 1962.
Levine, George. *The Realistic Imagination.* Chicago: University of Chicago Press, 1981.
Lukács, Georg. *Studies in European Realism.* Trans. Edith Bone. London: Hillway, 1950.
———. *Writer and Critic and Other Essays.* Trans. Arthur D. Kahn. New York: Grosset and Dunlap, 1970.
Lyotard, Jean-François. *The Postmodern Condition.* Trans. Geoff Bennington and Brian Massumi. Minneapolis: University of Minnesota Press, 1984.
Matthiessen, F. O. *Henry James: The Major Phase.* 1944. New York: Oxford University Press, 1963.
McHale, Brian. "Free Indirect Discourse: A Survey of Recent Accounts." *PTL* 3 (1977): 249–87.
Miller, James E. "Henry James in Reality." *Critical Inquiry* 2 (1976): 585–604.
Morot-Sir, Edouard. "L'Art des pronoms et le nommé dans l'oeuvre de Nathalie Sarraute." *Romanic Review* 72 (1981): 204–14.
———. "Texte, référence, déictique." *Texte* 1 (1982): 113–42.
Norrman, Ralf. *The Insecure World of Henry James's Fiction: Intensity and Ambiguity.* New York: St. Martin's Press, 1982.
Pascal, Roy. *The Dual Voice and its Functions in the Nineteenth Century European Novel.* Manchester: Manchester University Press, 1977.

Preminger, Alex, et al., eds. *The Princeton Encyclopedia of Poetry and Poetics*. Princeton: Princeton University Press, 1974.
Prendergast, Christopher. *The Order of Mimesis*. Cambridge: Cambridge University Press, 1986.
Proust, Marcel. *A la recherche du temps perdu*. 3 vols. Paris: Gallimard, 1954.
———. "A propos du style de Flaubert." *Nouvelle Revue Française* 14 (1920): 72–90.
Richard, Jean-Pierre. *Littérature et sensation*. Paris: Seuil, 1954.
Ricoeur, Paul. *The Rule of Metaphor: Multi-Disciplinary Studies in the Creation of Meaning in Language*. Trans. Robert Czerny, with Kathleen McLaughlin and John Costello. Toronto: University of Toronto Press, 1977.
Riffaterre, Michael. *Essais de stylistique structurale*. Paris: Flammarion, 1971.
Rorty, Richard. *The Consequences of Pragmatism*. Minneapolis: University of Minnesota Press, 1982.
———. *Philosophy and the Mirror of Nature*. Princeton: Princeton University Press, 1979.
Rowe, John Carlos. *The Theoretical Dimensions of Henry James*. Madison: University of Wisconsin Press, 1984.
Russell, Bertrand. *Logic and Knowledge*. London: George Allen and Unwin, 1956.
Sartre, Jean-Paul. *The Family Idiot*. Trans. Carol Cosman. Chicago: University of Chicago Press, 1981.
———. *L'Idiot de la famille. Gustave Flaubert de 1821–1857*. 3 vols. Paris: Gallimard, 1971–72.
Schor, Naomi, and Henry F. Majewski, eds. *Flaubert and Post-modernism*. Lincoln: University of Nebraska Press, 1986.
Schrag, Calvin. *Communicative Praxis and the Space of Subjectivity*. Bloomington: Indiana University Press, 1986.
Searle, John. *Speech Acts: An Essay in the Philosophy of Language*. Cambridge: Cambridge University Press, 1969.
Seltzer, Mark. *Henry James and the Art of Power*. Ithaca: Cornell University Press, 1984.
Sherrington, Robert. *Three Novels by Flaubert: A Study of Techniques*. New York: Oxford University Press, 1970.
Steele, H. Meili. "The Dangers of Structuralist Narratology: Genette's Misinterpretation of Proust." *Romance Notes* 26 (1986): 1–7.
Stern, J. P. *On Realism*. Boston: Routledge and Kegan Paul, 1973.
Stowe, William. *Balzac, Henry James and the Realistic Novel*. Princeton: Princeton University Press, 1983.
Thibaudet, Albert. *Gustave Flaubert*. Paris: Gallimard, 1935.
Todorov, Tzvetan. *La Poétique de la prose*. Paris: Seuil, 1971.
Ullman, Stephen. *Style in the French Novel*. New York: Barnes and Noble, 1964.
Ward, J. A. *The Search for Form: Studies in the Structure of James's Fiction*. Chapel Hill: University of North Carolina Press, 1967.
Watanake, H. "Past Perfect Retrospection in the Style of Henry James." *American Literature* 34 (1962): 165–81.

Weber, Samuel. *Unwrapping Balzac: A Reading of La Peau de chagrin.* Toronto: University of Toronto Press, 1979.
Wilson, R. B. J. *Henry James's Ultimate Narrative: The Golden Bowl.* St. Lucia: University of Queensland Press, 1981.
Yeazell, Ruth Bernard. *Language and Knowledge in the Late Novels of Henry James.* Chicago: University of Chicago Press, 1976.

Index

Amossy, Ruth, 24, 44, 140n, 141n
Armstrong, Paul, 145n
Auerbach, Erich, 5, 137n
Aurevilly, Barbey d', 13

Bachelard, Gaston, 33, 58
Balzac, Honoré de, works other than *Les Illusions perdues*
    Le Lys dans la vallée, 30
    La Peau de chagrin, 16
    Le Père Goriot, 40, 61, 140n
Barthes, Roland, 1, 14, 18, 36, 39, 44, 100, 143n
Beckett, Samuel, 18, 20, 50, 51, 65, 145n
Benveniste, Emile, 3, 149n
Bildungsroman, 15–17, 23–26, 35–36, 39–42, 44–49, 51–68, 72–73, 111–30
Blanchot, Maurice, 19–20
Brombert, Victor, 14, 16, 26, 67
Brooks, Peter, 7, 39–40, 61
Bruneau, Jean, 144n

Chatman, Seymour, 74, 102–4, 144n, 150–51n
Cohn, Dorrit, 101
Culler, Jonathan, 1, 14, 16–18, 51, 136n

Davidson, Donald, 136–37n
Deconstruction, 1–3
de Man, Paul, 2
Derrida, Jacques, 1–3, 22, 86, 97, 135n, 136n, 147–48n, 149n
Dumesnil, René, 13–14
Duquette, Jean-Pierre, 139n

Felman, Shoshana, 51
Flaubert, Gustave, works other than *L'Education sentimentale*
    Bouvard et Pécuchet, 68
    Correspondance, 38, 145
    Dictionnaire des idées reçues, 37
    Madame Bovary, 21, 44, 52
    Novembre, 51
Free indirect discourse, 28–31, 37, 54–55, 98–99, 101–2, 141n, 142n
Frege, Gottlob, 2–3, 89
Frye, Northrop, 49

Genette, Gérard, 45–46, 95, 144–45n
Gervais, David, 138n
Goodman, Nelson, 4
Gothot-Mersch, Claudine, 25, 142n

Greimas, A. J., 74, 146n
Grover, Phillip, 137n

Habegger, Alfred, 145n
Hacking, Ian, 136n, 151n
Hamon, Philippe, 5–6, 140n
Heidegger, Martin, 3, 4, 34, 93, 133, 136n
Herschberg-Pierrot, Anne, 38, 140–41n
History, 13, 20–22, 72–78

James, Henry, works other than *The Golden Bowl*
    criticism, 8–9, 71–72, 77
    The Portrait of a Lady, 76, 147n
    The Ambassadors, 76, 77, 82, 111–12, 146n, 147n, 151n
James, William, 82
Jameson, Fredric, 72
Jay, Gregory, 135n

Kadish, Doris, 138n
Kanes, Martin, 25
Kant, Immanuel, 57, 109, 113, 152–53n

Levine, George, 5
Locke, John, 72
Lukács, Georg, 18–19, 48, 53, 55, 140n
Lyotard, Jean-Francois, 139n, 150n

Matthiessen, F. O., 101
Miller, James E., 137n
Morot-Sir, Edouard, 3–4, 77, 88–89

Nietzsche, Friedrich, 97
Norrman, Ralf, 86, 145–46n, 149n

Prendergast, Christopher, 139n
Proust, Marcel, 22, 43, 63, 64

Realism, defined, 4–9
Reference, defined, 2–4
Richard, Jean-Pierre, 60
Ricouer, Paul, 3, 150n
Riffaterre, Michael, 140n
Rorty, Richard, 1–4, 136n
Rowe, John C., 1, 145n
Russell, Bertrand, 89–90, 148n

Sartre, Jean-Paul, 22, 29–30, 41–42
Saussure, Ferdinand de, 2–3, 7
Schrag, Calvin, 136n
Searle, John, 84, 89
Sherrington, Robert, 14
Stern, J. P, 5
Stowe, William, 7–8

Thibaudet, Albert, 42–43
Todorov, Tzvetan, 81

Wittgenstein, Ludwig, 78

Yeazell, Ruth, 7, 102, 112, 153n

Zola, Emile, 18

www.ingramcontent.com/pod-product-compliance
Lightning Source LLC
Chambersburg PA
CBHW021952290426
44108CB00012B/1036